Entering the Circle

The Secrets of
Ancient Siberian
Wisdom
Discovered by
a Russian
Psychiatrist

Entering
the Circle

Olga Kharitidi

HarperSanFrancisco
An Imprint of HarperCollins*Publishers*

HarperSanFrancisco and the author, in association with The Basic Foundation, a not-for-profit organization whose primary mission is reforestation, will facilitate the planting of two trees for every one tree used in the manufacture of this book.

A TREE CLAUSE BOOK

HarperCollins Web Site: http://www.harpercollins.com
HarperCollins,® ■,® HarperSanFrancisco,™ and A TREE CLAUSE BOOK®
are trademarks of HarperCollins Publishers Inc.
FIRST EDITION

Library of Congress Cataloging-in-Publication Data
Kharitidi, Olga.
   Entering the circle : the secrets of ancient Siberian wisdom discovered by a Russian
psychiatrist / Olga Kharitidi. — 1st ed.
     ISBN 0–06–251415–6 (cloth)
     ISBN 0–06–251417–2 (pbk.)
     1. Shamanism—Russia (Federation)—Siberia.   2. Shamans—Biography—Russia
(Federation)—Siberia.   I. Kharitidi, Olga.   II. Title.
   BF1611.K48   1996
   299'.4—dc20   96–10824

96 97 98 99 00 ❖HAD 10 9 8 7 6 5 4 3 2 1

Acknowledgments

I would like to express my deep gratitude and acknowledgment to the people who supported my work and assisted in the emergence of *Entering the Circle,* each in his or her own individual way. I gratefully thank Andrey Kogumayan, William H. Whitson, Marion Weber, Paula Gunn Allen, Maki Erdely, Wendy Gilliam, Dee Pye, Ansley, Kathy Sparkes, Rebecca Latimer, Winston O. Franklin, Barbara McNeil, Carol Rachbari, Elisabeth Hebron, JaneAnn Dow, Douglas Price-Williams, Carol Guion, and many others who participated in the appearance of this book.

My special appreciation is for my editor, Douglas H. Latimer, who, armed with his professionalism and inexhaustible sense of humor, was able to transform the supposedly hard and emotionally taxing dialogue between author and editor into one of inspirational creativity.

With all my love and gratefulness to my entire family.

If there was something in the air
If there was something in the wind
If there was something in the trees or bushes
That could be pronounced and once was overheard by animals,
Let this Sacred Knowledge be returned to us again.

ATHARVAVEDA (VII 66)

According to tradition, this hymn was offered in atonement for possible breaches in the conditions under which Sacred Knowledge was allowed to be transferred.

Author's Note

This is the true autobiographical account of a period in my life in which a strange chain of circumstances led me from my work in a psychiatric hospital in Novosibirsk, Siberia, into a series of remarkable shamanic experiences and revelations in the historically mystical region of the Altai Mountains. With minor exceptions, all of the events in the book took place as described. I have made only a few changes to protect the privacy of family and friends. The sections set apart in italics (written in the present tense) are taken directly from my journals. Dialogue was remembered and then later recorded as faithfully as possible. The drawings used throughout the book represent tattoos from a mummy unearthed in an ancient tomb in the Altai Mountains as well as other art from the same tomb.

Olga Kharitidi

Entering the Circle

Prologue

The rain finally stopped and the clouds cleared quickly away, blown by strong winds from the east. There was silence and an almost full darkness outside my window. Through the open balcony door, the fresh breeze carried a pleasant smell of wet leaves and moist asphalt into my apartment from the night street.

I turned off the light and walked onto the balcony for a last look at the evening sky. The entire city lay before me, reminding me of a giant passenger ship with lights glowing brightly from the portholes in its sides. Yet in reality this seemingly vast, luminescent city was only a little earth splinter, its lights insignificant beneath the thousands of brilliant stars that twinkled above it in the clear, peaceful night.

Suddenly, as I stood at the railing of my narrow balcony breathing the soft, fragrant air, one of the stars began to grow bigger and brighter than the others. Then the sky seemed to be torn apart, swirling violently as if the funnel of a huge tornado were rushing closer and closer, filling my vision.

I feel an enormous unknown power approaching, and I know I am being called once again to another place, another time. It is too late to escape or even to be afraid, although I am so accustomed to the "unusual" by now that I might not feel fear even if there were time for it.

Within a blink of my eyes, the entire scene changes. Where a moment before there was only the clear night sky, now bright sunlight fills my vision. I am floating high above the ground in a place I have never seen before. My mind works differently now, as if I were a new person, with no memory of the past. I am not afraid, just aware and responsive. I know I was brought here for a purpose. I trust this knowledge and wait.

As I float closer to the ground, I can see a grassy plain below me. The grass is spring green, tall, and full of newborn life, waving in the breeze. I can smell its fragrance, and this purely physical sensation helps me let go of other thoughts and centers me here.

Suddenly, loud drumming from my right commands my attention. My sense of smell has already pulled me into this new place, and now my sense of hearing deepens my connection with it. My body moves easily in the air, and I turn to the right toward the drumbeat. The scene that unfolds is one I could never have imagined.

Ten men, twenty-five to forty years old, their hair tied back in long ponytails, are dancing below me in a circle. Their clothes look strange to me, with muted, soft, earth tones decorated with patterns of geometric designs like nothing I have ever seen before. The drumming is constant, and while the men's movements are graceful, there is an unmistakable urgency in their dance. As I float closer to get a better look, I become aware of a woman lying in the middle of the circle. The men move and turn around her in their dance, a look of great intensity on their faces. There are no sounds except the insistent drumbeats.

At first I don't understand why the men look so unusual to me, but as I notice more and more details, I realize their faces show an awareness and connection with their ceremony that the people of our modern world have lost. I realize that they are ancient beings *and that I am experiencing something that happened many thousands of years ago.*

I am still floating above their dance circle, gradually moving downward toward the purpose of my being here. The woman who is the focal point of the dancing and drumming becomes more visible as I descend. Her lifeless figure is incredibly beautiful. The simplicity of her yellow-gray dress contrasts strongly with the elaborate jewelry gracing her neck and bodice. While the necklaces are crudely made, the jewels sparkling in them are exquisite. I know that she has just died.

I look around in an attempt to piece together what is happening and what I am to do here. My eyes are drawn to an old woman. She is sitting on a small wooden box near a yurtlike structure with a pointed roof of woven grass. She is smoking a pipe, moving her eyes constantly from the dance circle to the sky, her presence everywhere at once. Her physical age seems close to a hundred years, but her appearance is ageless. Her skin is dark and wrinkled, like dyed parchment exposed to a constant sun over many lifetimes. Her eyes are narrow, like those of many present-day Mongolians. They become even narrower as she squints, inhaling the smoke of her pipe.

Her part in this ceremony does not include the physical movement of the others. The rhythm of her being is much slower than that of the dancers. She breathes quietly, and sometimes she lifts her head slowly toward the sky as if she were expecting something. Just as I think this, she looks directly at me and I know she has seen me. There is a power in being recognized by this woman, and it creates a strange mixture of joy and fear within me.

I continue to float slightly above the ground. A question forms in my mind as I feel the woman focus and concentrate on me. "Who am I, and what am I here for?" Then the drum rhythm stops abruptly, and the men cease their dancing. As though of one body, they look up at me and begin chanting. Their language is unknown to me, yet somehow from among all the things they shout I recognize the words "White Goddess! The White Goddess is here!" It is not through an understanding of their language that I know these words. They are somehow instilled in my being, along with the old woman's penetrating gaze, which feels like waves continually passing through me.

My attention is suddenly directed back to the men, who have moved into a larger circle around the beautiful girl, making space so that I can easily descend to her side. Their heads are tilted upward, looking at me, and I feel their anticipation of what is to come. Nothing about it surprises me. If surprise is to come, it will be later, when I find myself standing once again on my balcony.

The body I am floating in is a huge woman's body, ten times normal size. White and weightless, I am like a cloud. I know from deep within my being that I have been brought here to bring this dead woman back to life.

I lower myself to the ground. As I reach her body, I touch the thick black braids that frame both sides of her soft, tawny face. I can sense that within her body she is hovering on some sort of boundary between life and death, and I know it is in my power to tilt the balance back toward life. I take her limp torso in my arms and lift her into a sitting position. Somehow, I know she must be kept in this position for the flow of life to come back into her body. When she is able to sit up by herself, I will know she is fully returned.

My hands begin moving around her head and breasts. My hands move by themselves, to the beat of an ancient ritual, and I am aware that these same movements and gestures were done thousands of years ago by others. The movements are restoring and balancing her energy, and when everything feels complete, I release her. Now she comes back slowly on her own, temporarily swimming between layers of unconsciousness and consciousness, her body healing itself on a path provided through me by some unknown force.

My work finished, I am raised by an unseen energy and float
above the scene once again. I fly higher and higher. Just as everything
below dissolves into distance, I see again the eyes of the old woman.
She is still looking at me, still smoking her pipe, totally aware of my
presence and who I am. I see gratitude in her face. In the moment
of change where everything dissolves, I recognize the old woman as
Umai, my old friend and teacher, in yet another manifestation.

Then I am again standing on my balcony, the night sky still brilliant before me. The transition between my journey and return to "reality," if indeed either is more real than the other, is quick and complete. Although I am a woman who lives in the modern twentieth-century world, by now I have learned to accept these experiences that were once so foreign to me.

Suddenly, I hear inside my head the words, "These people lived in a very distant past. In their rituals and ceremonies, performed many thousands of years ago, they knew precisely how to penetrate the barriers of space and time. They could reach the energy of people living in the future, and they knew how to integrate that energy into their ceremonies."

I remember how the funnel in the sky looked at the beginning of my journey and how my experience had shifted as I found myself floating above that ancient land. I hear the same voice say, "They knew how to travel on the ships of Belovodia," and I glimpse a small point of light moving quickly across the dark sky. It disappears within a few seconds. After it is gone, I continue to look up at the thousands of stars, among which one more mystery is hidden.

Now the journey is fully over, and I am once again in my little apartment in the middle of Siberia. Everything started here more than a year ago, when I woke up one seemingly normal winter morning and went to work, unaware that my whole life was about to change. I remember that day as clearly as if it had happened yesterday.

1

On this particular morning, like almost every other morning, my alarm went off at six o'clock sharp. The bus that would take me to the psychiatric hospital where I worked left exactly an hour later from a subway station a few blocks away. It was the last bus that would get me there on time, and I could not afford to miss it.

Today it was especially hard to force myself out of bed. My apartment was even colder than usual, and the sky outside was still dark, with sullen snow clouds obscuring the stars that might otherwise have brightened the night. The extreme cold in my room was a sure sign of a problem with the main furnace, and it meant I might not have heat again for days. Thinking of all this, I crawled reluctantly from under my warm blankets and prepared for a long day's work. After a quick breakfast of toast and coffee, more to warm myself than to furnish nourishment, I finished my morning chores.

I sighed as I closed the door to my apartment, thinking of the long trip I had to endure each morning to get to the work I loved. I entered the slippery, icy street, my frosty breath creating a path ahead of me in the still air. It had been snowing the entire night, and the janitor hadn't yet ventured out into the cold morning to shovel the mounds of windswept snow from the paths around the apartment building. It was difficult to make my way through the snowdrifts and frosty headwinds. I felt a cold chill run through my body, as much from the feeling of this dreary, somehow forbidding morning as from the wind and snow. The tall apartment buildings that surrounded me looked like huge dark, spiritless monsters. Only a few windows were lit among hundreds, each window a sign of human life in this Siberian stone jungle.

The sheltered subway stop was fifteen minutes away. I walked quickly with my head down, protecting myself as much as possible from the wind. The wet snow only appeared soft and beautiful; as it covered my face, hands, and clothes and then found its way to the un-covered skin of my neck, I again felt a cold chill run through my body.

My hurried steps created a rhythm, to which I added my usual win-ter morning's chant. The words were said just under my breath, in that singsong rhythm of preachers and spell weavers: "I want to get a seat today. I want to get a seat today." This time of year I would be very for-tunate to find a seat on the bus, and I desperately wanted the nap I would take if I had the chance.

It didn't happen. I arrived at the station to find a long line of people already waiting, ghostlike within their white snowy outlines. The slowly falling snow glistened in the dim white light of the street lamps and in the moving red taillights of white apparitions shaped like cars, their engines silenced by the wind. This morning as I approached the crowd, it melted together into a cloud of translucent common breath resembling a long, sinuously curling dragon, belching tobacco smoke and cursing loudly at the cold wind and the late bus.

I should have known there would be no hope of a seat or nap at this time of year because of all the men who traveled outside the city to the frozen river to fish. Each day my bus crossed the river Ob, one of the biggest rivers in Siberia. Its powerful wide stream divided my city, Novosibirsk, into two parts. Three long bridges had been built to con-nect the various districts of the city. It was after the first bridge was built, at the end of the last century, that the city began to grow. In win-ter the Ob is covered with thick ice, and the men who love to fish can walk all the way to the middle to cut their round openings. Then they sit with their comrades, telling stories and gossiping on the cold ice for hours, waiting for that first nibble from a hungry fish. The bus route follows the shore of the Ob until just before it reaches my hospital, and today, as nearly every other winter day, the early rising fishermen filled up the whole bus with their awkward equipment, sitting in the best seats, wearing long dark winter robes, and speaking in loud, raucous voices punctuated by curses.

I worked in a big psychiatric hospital with thousands of patients. The hospital lay outside the city because it had always been considered safer to locate such facilities well away from populated areas. After what seemed like much more than two hours of standing, swaying back and forth but otherwise immobilized by the pressing crowd in the freezing, unheated bus, I finally reached my stop at the hospital. I got out and walked quickly, trying to restore feeling to my numb legs.

Every day the same dreary picture greeted me: thirteen one-story buildings built in the style of old wooden army barracks, painted a yellow-green color, with heavy, badly rusted iron grates covering their tiny windows. This place provided the most important part of my life. This was my hospital.

Walking through the hospital yard, I saw about twenty people leaving the building that served as the kitchen. They carried big metal buckets full of breakfast in their hands, and they hurried back to their wards in a hopeless attempt to keep their morning tea and gruel warm. I could hardly see them because it was still so dark, but I could hear their steps distinctly on the icy snow, accompanied by the metallic sounds of their buckets as they took separate paths to their different buildings. The same gruel was served every day. It was the only food available to us. The huge metal buckets, with their two metal handles and flat lids, reminded me of what one might use to feed inmates in a prison.

There were some patients whose mental state allowed them to do menial work within the hospital grounds. These privileged few wore identical long-sleeved gray jerseys with their ward numbers printed in big numerals on the back. The women's heads were covered by shawls;

the men had shaved heads. Some had been my patients for a long time. Despite the darkness, many of them recognized me and shouted friendly greetings. Others, new and unfamiliar to me, were silent.

I arrived at my ward and prepared for the daily morning conference. I always approached these conferences with tension. The nurses would brief me on the events of the night, and I had to be ready for anything. Today was no different, and I caught myself anticipating the many possible problems that might have arisen.

First, I heard from the night report how an orderly I had hired only a month ago had gotten drunk and had unmercifully beaten a harmless, senile patient who had only refused to perform a meaningless request. The orderly had kicked the old man again and again with his heavy army boots, sending him to the emergency surgical clinic with a ruptured spleen.

I hoped the poor fellow would survive. Somehow I felt it was my fault it had happened, yet I knew it was not. Most of the people who were willing to work as orderlies were men who had served time in prison, and they often brought their drug and alcohol addictions with them. They replaced one another regularly. One would be suspended from work after some criminal incident, and another would take his place, with the same face dulled by alcohol and the same cynical mind— not a good combination for the patients they took care of. I had little choice in who I hired, and at least it made it easier to know there was really no way I could have protected my patient. He was in surgery at that very moment, and I said a quick silent prayer for him.

The nurse reported next about a new patient who had been delivered to the hospital by the police at three o'clock in the morning. I read the policeman's report on the young man:

The patient was found in the forest, twenty-five kilometers from the city. He was running down the railroad tracks toward an oncoming train. He couldn't explain anything after his detention.

He answered no questions and was unable to connect with what was around him. He didn't even realize we had taken him.

Clothes: Army uniform, dirty and torn.

Documents: Certificate, Soldier of the Soviet Army.

He speaks to himself. It becomes understandable from some of his words that he sees aliens from a UFO all around him.

I was curious to see him, but it was time for my morning rounds in the men's ward. I would have to visit him later.

Eighty mentally sick men lived in ward rooms dimly lit with blue ceiling lights. They all wore identical, soiled, gray, uniform-style pajamas with vertical black stripes. Five to ten patients were housed together in each room. They had no privacy, since their rooms were all without doors. One large room for chronic patients held more than twenty men. Women orderlies tried to wash and clean the ward, but it was impossible to get rid of the pungent smell of human sweat mixed with urine, medicine, and unpleasant stuffiness. This was the regular odor of my work, and I had become used to it long ago.

My patients were all so familiar to me that they felt almost like family. I knew each person's life history from earliest childhood to the point where mental disease had cut off his expectations, career, and family—his whole life up to that very moment—and isolated him in what was called the "crazy house."

Each patient was different. As I made my rounds, one asked me to reduce his dose of medicine because he already felt so much better. Another didn't even hear me coming, because his mind had room only for his inner voices. Someone else simply laughed quietly in the corner. The one consistent thing about them was the pale, almost ghostly quality of their faces, with dark circles under their eyes. These people never saw the sky or breathed fresh air.

I moved from one patient to another, noticing changes in their medical conditions, giving the usual daily treatment recommendations to the nurses, answering questions. I thought briefly again about the new patient. "A soldier," I thought to myself. "That's very interesting. Could the horrors of army life have led this man to fake a mental disease?"

Playing mentally ill was a familiar trick that many men used to get out of the army. Males were usually conscripted into the army right after high school, as eighteen-year-old boys. Coming from secure home environments, they were completely unprepared for the shocking behavior they encountered. They experienced taunts, humiliations, and even beatings from veteran soldiers. This was the unwritten army law. If you didn't do it to others, they would do it to you. Many were unable to accept it. Some who couldn't handle it actually did develop serious mental illnesses and had to be shut away. Others, seeing this, preferred the relative safety of being locked in the mental hospital and so pretended to be ill.

I entered the room for the newly arrived patients. I could see from my first glance that this soldier was unquestionably sick. He sat in the corner, rigid with fear, looking more like a scared animal than a human being. His entire body displayed incredible tension. I never ceased to wonder where this impossible energy of the mentally ill came from. How did their bodies create it?

The same energy that for now immobilized the soldier could also provide an incredibly violent physical strength that often led patients to hurt themselves or others. I had seen variations of this picture replayed time after time, patient after patient. This poor fellow's clothes were exactly as the policeman had described them, dirty and torn. The night staff had been unable to change them without doing more harm than good, so this would become a task for the day shift. Even now, sitting nervously on the floor, he was still ripping at them. The clothes were made of strong cloth designed to survive the harsh conditions of a soldier's life, and it would not have been possible for him to tear them in his normal state of mind.

He continued to destroy his few remaining possessions as I watched. His blank, light blue eyes gazed steadily at nothing. Our ward might contain his body, but the rest of his being was somewhere totally beyond it.

His lips whispered some indecipherable words. I asked him a few necessary questions without expecting any answers. I did not have access to whatever his "reality" might be at that moment, so I thought about the dosage of the injection I would give him. I knew that later, when he became lucid, he would describe to me the images and experiences he was now having.

His name was Andrey, and he looked about seventeen or eighteen years old. His body was very thin. Maybe he had lost weight due to the poor nutrition that was standard in the army. His light brown hair had been closely shaved by the army barbers, and it was only about an inch long over his entire head. It made his face look vulnerable and open. His was still very much a child's face, with an expression of great fear on it. He was just a boy whose mind had been totally overwhelmed by the traumatic experiences that now would probably affect him for the rest of his life. For now, a medium intravenous dose of Haloperidol should be enough to calm him down and begin his return to reality.

My next patient was Sergey, a handsome, young, sturdily built fellow who outwardly appeared ready to go home soon. He looked cheerful, spoke to me openly, and talked critically about his experiences while he was sick. He had been very helpful in the ward work. But maybe everything was just a little bit too good, a little bit too cheerful, a little bit too open. He passionately wanted to go home to be with his lovely, young wife, but I knew that a major portion of his psychosis was connected with pathological jealousy.

As always in the case of potentially dangerous patients, the hospital's chief medical officer had been called in for consultation. He had prescribed a combination of drugs to suppress Sergey's conscious will, which in turn would force him to speak the truth. I had not given these medicines to him yet, even though they would surely have told me his real state of mind concerning his wife.

This sort of decision always created a moral dilemma for me. If I were Sergey, how would I feel if somebody, without my permission, entered my psyche through drugs to get answers to any questions they might want to ask? My negative opinion of this process never changed, and it disturbed me every time these drugs were prescribed.

Hopefully, I could find a different way to deal with Sergey's case. Anyway, I already knew I must meet with his wife and insist they get a divorce. I needed to make her understand that she had to be as far away from him as possible. His illness would always be dangerous, and there was too great a possibility that he might kill her, or someone else, in an irrational fit of jealous rage. Unfortunately, I had already seen the tragic finality of too many similar stories.

As I came to a temporary close in my thoughts about Sergey, I heard the nurse calling me back to my office. The mother of my new patient, the young soldier named Andrey, had just arrived. Someone from the army administration office had contacted her, and she had traveled here immediately. Most relatives, even mothers, did not usually come to the crazy house so quickly.

She had a typical Russian manner. She and her son strongly resembled each other, with the same simple, open face and plain features. The nervous motions of her hands also reminded me of her son, as she stood crumpling her dark winter country dress, afraid to sit without my permission. I knew from reading Andrey's papers that she lived in a nearby village with her husband and two sons, one of whom was now in this hospital.

It was obvious she had never been to a psychiatric clinic. She didn't yet understand at all what had happened to her older son. She was actually glad he had been able to come back so quickly from the army and was grateful for his safe return. She would no longer have to worry about him for the two years she had expected him to be gone. She did not yet understand the difference between schizophrenia and influenza.

Her first question was that of any caring mother: "Tell me, doctor, how soon will he get better?"

If I had told her the full truth immediately, I would have answered, "Never." Instead I said, "It will probably take about two weeks to bring him back." Her face transformed into happiness. Later I would have to try to explain that I meant he would recover from his present acute psychosis in two weeks, but that when he came back to her he would be different from before. Maybe only a little different at first, but there would be more changes in his personality and behavior as time went by. He would never again be the normal boy she remembered. How could I tell her that an evil that destroys minds and souls without discrimination had already made its home in him? I knew from my experience that schizophrenia was a claw no one could pull out.

Experience also told me she would not believe me at first. She would wait expectantly for her son to return from the hospital and to recover fully with the support of his loving family. She and his father would expect him to help again with the chores at their small country home. For a while things might seem almost normal, until one day the claw would attack his body again, making him run down a different set of railroad tracks toward some other moving train. Something like this would certainly happen, and after that his mother would live in fear of the time when her other son, her baby, also had to be sent off to serve in the army. But for now the mother had heard enough, and she left to tell her husband and son the good news that Andrey would return to them in two weeks.

This helpless feeling of professional weakness, my lack of omnipotence as a doctor, was one of the most difficult aspects of my work. I never got used to the fact that I often had to admit partial or full defeat to the diseases I was fighting. I did not know if other specialties of medical doctors felt this as regularly, but it was a well-known occupational hazard for psychiatrists. There were no drugs, no medicines, no quick surgical techniques for bringing back a patient's mind. Now I took a moment to close my eyes and breathe deeply, clearing my mind. As I opened my eyes again, I heard a knock at my office door.

Grateful for the interruption, I called out, "Come in." My friend Anatoli entered, and I was glad to see someone I enjoyed talking to. "Hi!" he said. "Shall we have lunch and a cup of tea?"

The morning had passed quickly, and I hadn't realized it was already noon. This was a favorite time for the hospital staff, as it gave us a chance to visit in each other's wards, chatting and eating the lunches we had brought from home. These generally were just simple sandwiches or salads with a strong cup of coffee or tea. It was only on special days, such as birthdays or national holidays, that we might bring our favorite treats like dessert or caviar, since they were too expensive to purchase regularly.

I liked Anatoli. He was young and physically fit, with brown hair and blue eyes. His creativity, intelligence, and sensitivity made him one of our best doctors. We often talked about him. His professors and colleagues had expected him to have a very good career in psychiatry, but this had not yet happened. I had often thought of bringing this up with him, but the time had never seemed quite right. Today I finally decided to ask him about it.

He was sitting on the couch in front of me with the traditional cup of tea, wearing the obligatory white hospital gown. His eyes were hidden, as usual, behind tinted glasses.

"You know, Anatoli, many people believe you are a psychiatric genius. Can I ask why your career does not reflect that yet?"

He took my comments as a compliment, with visible pleasure. "But I do have a very good career," he replied. Then with an ironic grin he said, "But I guess you know this is not a psychiatric hospital?"

My facial expression didn't show any surprise, because by now I was used to his trick of playing with meanings.

"This is not a hospital at all," he continued. "It is a giant crazy ship, and we who are the crew actually believe that we work here as medical doctors. We even believe we can treat people and cure them. But I don't think it is a great idea to make a career on a crazy ship. All we can do is navigate blindly on the ocean of reality all around us, believing we know what we are doing. We will continue navigating in directions unknown to us, because we cannot stop. Each of us here has made the choice to float through reality on this ship, and we cannot leave it now. Because this is the safest place for us to be if we think we are medical doctors, really able to treat people who are supposed to be crazy."

"Don't you think there is any escape for us at all?" I asked, understanding the ruse he was using to avoid a serious answer to my question.

"Well, I think perhaps there might be one vehicle we could take to escape into reality. You can see it right now. Look here!"

With a sardonic grin, he gestured to the window. Through it I could see the familiar shape of the big, old, broken-down trolley car that sat in the yard outside our building. It sat without wheels, its rust-corroded body complete with metal antlers pointing vainly up to the sky, reaching for wires that were no longer there. Nobody knew why this trolley car had been left in the middle of the hospital grounds.

Anatoli was laughing now. He still had not given a direct answer to my question about his career, and his eyes had a Mephistophelian gleam to them. "Thank you very much for the tea and conversation. And now I must go back to work and complete some more passenger— sorry, I mean patient—histories."

2

Later, as I was completing my paperwork and dreading the long bus trip back to my little apartment, the phone rang in my office. I picked it up and heard "Hello, Olga!" in a voice I recognized immediately as Anna's. Anna was a medical doctor, and we had been close friends for many years. I had become adept at sensing the many different moods of her complex personality through the sounds and rhythms of her voice. Today she sounded tired and worried.

As usual, for a while we chattered about nothing and everything. Anyone listening to us might have found our conversation trivial, but every time we talked, even about simple things, I rediscovered the importance of our friendship. There was always a phrase, an emotion, or simply a surge of energy between us that left me feeling joyful and alive. I knew it was the same for her.

The main reason for her call today became clear when she asked if I could make time to see her neighbor, who feared he had a serious mental problem. I couldn't refuse her request, so I asked her to send him to my office the next day at three o'clock. Anna had never visited me at the hospital, so I gave her directions and I marked the appointment in my calendar. We made a date to see each other soon and then said our good-byes.

The next day, at exactly three P.M., the day nurse brought a young man to my office. He stood hesitantly in my doorway.

"How do you do, doctor. I am Nicolai. Your friend, Anna Anatolievna, referred me to you."

Nicolai was a young Siberian with a handsome Mongolian face. With age, faces such as his were often dominated by a hard masculine strength. This man was still young enough to show hints of shyness and sensitivity, both of which were particularly apparent at the moment. He was clearly embarrassed and ill at ease to be standing in a psychiatrist's office.

Apart from his nervousness, the young Siberian standing in front of me certainly didn't look mentally ill. Still, I guessed he must have felt he was in serious trouble to have taken Anna into his confidence and then to have come here of his own free will. In my professional experience, I had discovered that very few people were willing to seek psychiatric help on their own. There was a tremendous stigma attached to any hint of mental abnormality. This not only dissuaded people from getting help but also led those who did so to try every means possible to keep it secret. If their situation became known by their friends or colleagues, it inevitably created social discrimination.

Nicolai moved forward and stood in the middle of my small office, still looking awkward and unsure of himself. I told him to make himself comfortable, gesturing him to the chair in front of my desk. I watched him as he went to it and sat down. He looked like a factory worker. He wore a neat dark gray suit, white shirt, and black tie. I could tell he perceived our meeting as a very official event. He sat nervously on the edge of the chair. I didn't hurry him but simply waited for him to tell his story. After a short silence to collect his thoughts, he began.

"Thank you for seeing me. The reason I am here started about a month ago."

He spoke Russian with a slight mountain accent I found pleasant. Anna had told me he came from Altai, an isolated, ethnically different region with its own language. I was not surprised to hear him give a typically Russian name, for all native peoples were given Russian names when they applied for internal passports from the Soviet state. It was a purposeful evil, intended to hasten the destruction of their cultures by deliberately erasing the heritage that lived in their names.

Nicolai didn't look at me as he spoke. It was clear that he still felt very embarrassed but that he had made a commitment to himself to talk to me and was determined to fulfill it. Undoubtedly it was difficult for him to open up his mind to a stranger, and he feared my reaction to what he was about to say.

"This thing began for me when my mother asked me to come home to my village in Altai." The expression on his face showed that he was reluctant to speak about his village. This was common. Many youths who came to work in the city preferred to hide their country origins for fear of being ridiculed. He continued slowly.

"My uncle, Mamoush, had become very sick, and my mother needed me to help nurse him. We were his only relatives, and he had lived alone, apart from the other people of the village. I had never been interested in spending any time with him, but I could not refuse my mother's request. I had no choice but to take a vacation without pay and go home.

"I spent ten days there. My uncle died on the fifth day. He was eighty-four years old, and like most of our people of his age he knew his time had come. He had no interest in trying to live any longer. In our village we believe that anyone of his age has already lived a complete life and would want to die. I had never had much love for my uncle, so I had no desire to change anything unless it was to help him move on quickly so I could return to my life in the city."

As Nicolai went on his voice trembled, and he paused longer and longer between sentences. All the while, he continued to emphasize that he had never been close to his uncle. I couldn't help wondering why he was still so nervous. His sensitive personality wasn't enough by itself to explain being so affected by the death of an aged relative he had hardly even known. I knew his story didn't fit together yet, but I didn't ask questions or interrupt. My job for now was just to listen and let him continue his story in his own way.

Nicolai continued to ramble, telling me how difficult it had been for his mother to take care of his dying uncle and what he, Nicolai, had done to support her. Then he shared some opinions with me about the nature of his uncle's disease, switching from one possible malady to another. I could see that his fears were getting in the way of his desire to be healed and that he was trying to find the courage to tell me the real essence of his story.

I finally decided to interrupt him, in an attempt to bring him back to the reason he had come here. "Nicolai, you suggested that whatever it was that you wanted to talk to me about began about a month ago?"

He agreed without either speaking or looking at me, simply nodding his head up and down.

"What happened after your uncle's death?"

"Well, it is a strange story. . . ."

"I have heard many strange stories. What is so strange about yours?"

"Do you believe in shamans?" he asked tentatively.

Now it suddenly struck me that perhaps I, not he, might be the one in trouble. I knew almost nothing at all about shamanism. The word *shaman* had a very negative meaning in our society, as an unhealthy symbol of primitive cultural and spiritual beliefs. I had to be very careful with my answer.

"Unfortunately, I know only that shamanism had to do with the old religion of the Siberian peoples, long before Christianity. That is all I know. But I believe in the existence of people called shamans."

Gradually, still without looking at me, he seemed to understand that I was accepting his words without judging them. His body relaxed into a softer posture, and his voice sounded less nervous.

"My uncle was a shaman," he continued. "Because of that, I did not like to spend time with him. He lived in solitude on the edge of the village. Many who lived there believed he had very strong shamanic powers, but nobody was sure he used these powers only for the proper things. And maybe they were right. People were afraid of him, and they avoided him except when they needed his help for their problems and diseases.

"I never was interested in such things myself. From the time I was very young, my only wish was to leave him, and even my village, as soon as I could. You know there is nothing to do in the country, especially in the winter. It is cold and boring. I never doubted that I would go to the city right after I graduated from high school. I wanted to serve in the army but didn't pass the medical examination. My vision is terrible. So, you might understand how happy I was to find my present job. I have been working here for almost a year now, and I have already been promised an apartment for next year. It is rare to have this happen so soon. For now, of course, I still live in a dormitory."

I knew that as soon as young men and women got jobs at a plant, their names would be put on a waiting list to get their own apartments. Sometimes it could take up to twenty years for a name to come to the top of the list. Occasionally a name might even get lost, and the happy reward of a private place to live might never happen at all. These unfortunate people would live out their working lives in dormitories where three or four people shared a single small room. Sometimes as many as fifteen or twenty rooms would share one small kitchen area, one shower, and one toilet. I understood how much it would mean to Nicolai to be promised an apartment so soon.

Nicolai continued, "I have a girlfriend, and we are planning to get married. So, you could say that my life's dreams have started to come true. Now I am afraid everything may be lost. I really need your help, doctor. I am ready to do anything, to take any medicines to restore my health. To restore my sanity."

He looked at me with a desperate hope I rarely saw in my patients. It was still difficult for me to piece his story together. His shamanic uncle had died, and now he feared he was mentally ill. His problem was not yet clear to me. I tried to postpone a conclusion of some kind of psychosis, even if what I had heard so far of his story tempted me toward such a conclusion.

Hesitatingly, he resumed talking. "I fell sick the day after my uncle's death. While he was dying, he had asked me to spend time with him alone. I was not happy about this at all, but I agreed because it was his last request. He lived in a small dark house without electricity. He had a collection of very strange things there: half-dead plants, stones (some with pictures on them), his drum, tattered clothes. Everything in his small house was unusual. I was frightened, yet I felt I had no choice but to spend his last days alone with him.

"Then my uncle began to speak to me about power—shamanic power. The first time, he talked more than two hours about it. I was not attentive. It sounded to me as if he was having some sort of dying fantasy, so I simply tried to be polite to him. We had many other conversations. I don't remember much except the very last one.

"It happened late one night. His illness had grown worse and worse, but he hadn't let me invite anyone else to be with us. His breathing became rapid and heavy. His speech became interrupted, and he seemed confused. I knew his end was near. Finally, he asked me to come close to his bed. The room was dark. Only the corner where his high, narrow wooden bed was placed was dimly lit by the flame of a single candle, burning on a small table amidst strange amulets and dried herbs.

"My uncle lay covered by a warm blanket made from multicolored scraps of different fabrics. When I drew near, he grasped my hand roughly in his own hot dry hands. From somewhere, his voice suddenly found great strength and clarity. He stared at me intensely. His whole being had changed so dramatically that for a moment I actually thought he had rid himself of his disease.

"Slowly and with great concentration, as if he might have been trying to hypnotize me, he said, 'Shamanic powers live with us in this world, and they must be left in this world. I am dying, and my power won't follow where I am going. I give it to you, because this is what has been decided by the spirits.'

"As he spoke I experienced a severe cramp in the hand he was so desperately holding. It felt as though a fire flashed through my body. I was too stunned for a moment even to notice that in that same instant my uncle had died. My state of mind was completely strange to me. I could not, and still cannot, fully describe what happened. I understand that this might be necessary for you to diagnose what's wrong with me, but I don't know what else to say. I tried to throw light on my problem by reading some books about psychiatry, but I had to give them up. It was much too difficult for me to understand the words."

He had almost been reliving his experience as he described it. His left hand had seemed to cramp when he talked about it. His face was now sweating, as if he had heard his dead uncle's voice again while talking to me.

"Let's take a little break from talking about your uncle. Maybe you can tell me a little more of your life in the city?"

He accepted my suggestion with obvious relief. "What would you like me to tell you?" He shrugged his shoulders indecisively.

"Tell me about your work, the workers at your plant. How do they relate to you?"

"Well. Very well."

I looked at him silently. He was motionless, sitting very straight on the edge of his chair. His posture showed a great deal of tension.

"They are good people, but they are very different from the people in my home village."

"What are the differences?"

"Well, it's difficult to say. I've never really thought about it. I've just felt it. They drink a lot, even at work. My people also like vodka, but they would never be as rude after a few drinks, or even after many drinks."

I imagined this sensitive young man among his coarser fellow plant workers. Well, at least part of his dream of moving to the city hadn't been as lovely as he had expected.

"Are you trying to be like them?"

"No, I don't think so. I realize that I have to get used to being here, though. It was my wish to live in a big city, but I expected a lot more from it. I guess I still believe it can be a lot more. I only need to get used to being here. And I need to be healthy."

After a brief pause, which seemed to help him collect his strength, Nicolai continued.

"After my uncle's death I had a very high fever for five days. I did not eat, I did not speak. I did not even remember who I was. In my delirium I saw him all the time. Thanks to a local district doctor, who came to see me and gave me some injections, I recovered from the fever. I forgot everything that had come to me in my sickness, and although I still felt very weak, I returned to work.

"Then I got better and better physically, but at the same time something began happening to my mind. I started to hear my uncle's voice demanding that I remember my dreams. Now his voice comes to me without warning, anytime, anywhere. It comes when I am speaking with people, and when I am on the bus among strangers. I become deeply frightened when this happens, and I know I must seem crazy. I feel panic and want to run away. It is becoming so bad, I am afraid I may be fired from my job." After a long, deep sigh, he asked if he might smoke.

Normally I would not let a patient smoke in my office. In Nicolai's case, I decided to break the rule. I felt it would help him be comfortable and open up. He took a pack of cigarettes without filters from his suit pocket and frantically looked for his matches, his hands moving quickly from pocket to pocket without finding them.

I stood up and went to the corner of the room opposite my desk. From the top of the refrigerator I took the matches and the tea saucer that occasionally substituted as an ashtray and handed them to him.

The small hinged opening at the top of my window was too high for me to reach, so before going back to my desk, I used a long pine stick to open it a little bit. The stick had a carved human head at one end. It had been made for me a few years earlier by an elderly patient who for twenty years had believed he was God and who had tried incessantly to create people from wood. The man had died the year before, old and alone like so many of our patients. There were no relatives to bury him, so the hospital sent his body to the medical school to be used for studying anatomy.

I remembered that when I began medical school, one of the hardest things for me emotionally was having to dissect the old, thin, often decrepit corpses. Eventually, I had no choice but to relate to them as tools for science, trying to forget that they had once been people who had lived the ends of their lives alone, with no one to care for them or give them comfort at the moment they died. Even at the medical school, where they became objects in the name of science, their lifeless bodies were denied respect.

Freezing cold air burst in through the window's narrow opening and swirled through my office. Nicolai moved his chair away from my desk and smoked with deep inhalations.

"What am I going to do with this man?" I wondered. I knew I had all the resources I needed to begin an effective psychiatric strategy to diagnose and treat him. If Nicolai had been an official, legally admitted patient, I would have been more or less required to order a series of laboratory tests that would tell me if he suffered from the aftereffects of some unknown fever, manifested through a residual organic psychosis, with possible episodes of seizure. But in this case I could be more flexible, so I decided to try something different first. I would do what I felt was correct for Nicolai. Depending on the outcome, I could always use a more traditional psychiatric therapy later.

I asked him if he was willing to try an experiment. He nodded his head in agreement, and I asked, "Do you think you could hear your uncle's voice again, in my presence?"

He inhaled deeply again, and it was obvious that the cigarette had made him more comfortable. "I think I can, but I don't know how to make it happen. It always comes by itself, without my willing it."

"Perhaps we can do it together."

"I agree to try."

I pushed the hidden button on the floor near my desk, signaling for the nurse to come into my office. The button had been put there originally for emergencies with violent patients, but we usually used it as a form of communication between different stations in the hospital.

When the nurse arrived I asked her to walk Nicolai to the hypnotary, the room where we carried out hypnosis, and to wait for me there. He put out his cigarette, stood up, and took his short black sheepskin coat from the nurse.

I watched them from the window as they walked through the snow to the hypnotary. They were talking to each other, and I wondered what about. The nurse was a professional. She had retired a few months ago but then had decided to return to work to help support her three daughters. It was common for parents to help support their children even after they started working at their own jobs. This nurse, who was both conscientious and frugal, managed to buy new clothes for her daughters almost every two months. It sometimes cost more than half her salary to do this, yet she did it willingly. I was glad she was back.

I had just finished filling out and signing ward papers and was about to go to the hypnotary when the doctor on duty called me from the reception ward. "Olga," he said, "I am admitting a very serious patient to your women's ward. She has been coming here periodically for twenty years. The diagnosis is schizophrenia. She was last admitted to our clinic two years ago. Now she is in the last degrees of cachexia [physical exhaustion]. It appears she hasn't really eaten in more than a month because of the voices that fill her mind. I'll prepare all the prescription orders for the nurses tonight, but I'd really like you to see her and her husband before you leave today."

"When will she be at the ward?" I asked.

"In an hour and a half," he replied.

I agreed to see her and was relieved that I would still have time to work with Nicolai first.

Our doctors had put a lot of their own efforts into creating the hypnotary. It had already been built when I began working at the hospital, and it was a miracle that it existed at all. Over and over again, I had heard the stories of the dedicated doctors who had made legends of themselves by supplying the equipment, supplies, furniture, and carpeting to create this important facility. It could never have been done through government channels. The hypnotary was crucial to my work, and I always felt comfortable there.

I entered the darkened room quietly, the plush carpet allowing me to move with soundless steps. A small red lamp sat on the floor in each corner of the room. The room's silence and the faint red glow of the lamps helped me make the necessary mental and emotional trip beyond the sounds and images of the world outside.

The nurse had already prepared Nicolai. He was reclining in a soft, deep armchair in the middle of the room, wearing only his white shirt and pants. His suit jacket, tie, and boots had been taken to another room by the nurse, who would have them waiting for him at the end of the session. He looked relaxed and did not even notice my arrival. I quietly walked over to him and slowly let the back of the armchair down.

"We can start now, Nicolai. I need you to answer my questions honestly and as accurately as possible. If you don't have an answer, don't try to think one up. Our success does not depend on the number of questions you answer. It depends on a different quality. And we don't have to discuss what that is but only trust it, knowing that it is already present and true for us and that we may be guided by it." My words were deliberately obscure, because I needed to confuse his mind in order to create an opening for my words to enter his unconscious.

Nicolai closed his eyes, and his facial muscles became more relaxed as I consciously spoke to him in a deeper and deeper voice, speaking more slowly and quietly with each word.

"Now I am going to ask your body a question that doesn't require your answer, Nicolai. You don't even have to listen. I need to get an agreement from your body that it will help protect you from stress during our work. Now I'm speaking directly to your body, asking it to cooperate with us in protecting you. And I'm waiting for an answer." His left hand gave a small tremor, and I knew from my experience that it was a sign of agreement.

"Thank you," I responded in acknowledgment.

I continued, "Nicolai, in the past there have been many times when I have tried to recall an important memory but found it impossible to do so. The more I focused, the more unavailable my memory became. I tried again and again, until I became absolutely exhausted. Then I gave up and relaxed. Shortly thereafter, the image I sought came to me from my unconscious. This phenomenon was what first led me to understand the power of the unconscious mind and to realize that it can help us immensely if we learn how to communicate with it.

"As I speak to you now, you may not understand some of the things I talk about. Don't be concerned. It is not necessary for your conscious mind to know the meaning of my words, so don't interrupt the calm and relaxed state that is expanding inside your mind and body by trying to understand them. Your unconscious will know. I want to enlist the support of that power that has been speaking to you in order to teach you something important. This may not make sense to you yet, but my intention is to help you understand.

"Do you remember the last time you heard your uncle's voice? Please answer yes by moving your left hand or no by moving the right one. Was it on Monday?"

Nicolai's right hand moved slightly. "Tuesday?" No. "Wednesday?. . . "

When I reached Friday, the left hand moved.

"Place yourself where it happened. Is it dark where you are?"

No.

"You are in a well-lighted place. I think this is your workplace. You are speaking with a colleague." Carefully observing the response from his hand, I continued as it made little movements of agreement. "The time now is just before your uncle speaks. You can remain calm and relaxed, because we are in charge of this experience and nothing bad can happen.

"You are at the point in your memory where you can hear the voice of your uncle. No one from your work notices anything. The colleagues you were talking to go away, dissolve. Your attention shifts from them to your uncle's voice."

Nicolai's face became tense. He breathed more deeply and quickly. I reached forward and placed my hand on the middle of his chest, saying, "Now my hand breathes together with your lungs, and we can bring this rhythm down, slowly and calmly—gradually, together."

He calmed down, and said softly, almost in a whisper, "I hear him. . . ."

"Listen to everything his voice tells you. Be calm and sure. My hand is here with your breath, and you can get help from me or stop any time you want. But you won't need to stop, for you are protected and safe."

Nicolai spoke softly, "He is not frightening me now. He is different from before."

"Stop talking to me, Nicolai. You did not come here to speak. You came to listen. So do it now. I appreciate your sharing with me, but not right now. We will do that later. For now, just try to remember everything your uncle says, and be open to it."

I stood over him in the reclined armchair for half an hour, my hand on his chest. It was fairly dark in the room, but I could see his face. It was relaxed, and at first it looked as though he was sleeping. Gradually, as he began to relive his memory, his expression became more active. His eyes began to move quickly under their closed lids. He was obviously seeing intense images. All the emotions he was experiencing were reflected in his face. I saw him wondering, expressing curiosity at first, then deep sadness, and I thought he might start crying. I sensed he was very far away, experiencing something important in his memory. I guided his breathing with my hand, slowing him down, prepared to wake him up if his emotional state appeared dangerous. Otherwise, I would let him return on his own when he was done.

Finally, he took a long, very deep breath and announced, "I have completed my journey. I am ready to come back now."

His voice sounded stronger and more sure of itself. I spoke to him again.

"Now I ask you to be attentive to my words, Nicolai. Gradually you will recall how we first met this afternoon, when you came to the hospital. You probably feel very different now, because you have a new memory inside you. When you return from your journey and come back to my office, you will notice these changes. Then you will remember what happened to you, and you will tell me about it. When I take my hand off your chest, you will open your eyes and be present here again."

I noticed his left hand was tightly squeezing the armrest, and I touched it softly to help him relax. I walked to the wall, turned on the overhead light, and pressed the button to call in the nurse. The red lamps turned off automatically.

I could now see the paintings that had been donated to the hospital by the Siberian Gallery of Fine Art. It was always a small miracle to me that such fine paintings had found their way to this unlikely place. There were some beautiful landscapes on the walls, but the most special painting to me was an oil portrait of a young woman with hair parted in the middle who was wearing rich, lace-trimmed clothes from some past century. She had a kind, reassuring face, and when I worked there, I felt almost as if she supported me.

The nurse helped Nicolai stand up and put his jacket back on. I threw my fur coat over my shoulders and began the walk back to my office. I was quite satisfied with the session. It had gone very well, and it felt right to have tried to resolve Nicolai's inner conflict without pharmacology. I hoped the experience would prove to be what he needed to settle this family relationship that had appeared to him in such a mythological-religious form.

Nicolai entered my office looking serious and somehow different. Part of his transformation was that now he seemed completely relaxed, not even caring how he looked. He held his tie in his hand and sat at ease in the same chair he had occupied so nervously before.

"I want to thank you for your assistance. I was given a very important message. It changed many feelings inside of me."

I listened attentively, noticing at the same time how my own feeling of self-esteem was growing. I started to think I was a very lucky therapist to hear such words from my patients so often.

"I was glad to help you. I hope it will allow you to live your life more easily and be successful."

"But everything has changed, doctor. I think that I must become a shaman."

I was stunned. I sat immobile in my chair, trying to keep the same blank expression on my face as I listened to him. But my feeling of self-esteem plummeted lower and lower, turning into shame. How could I have let this happen? This man had come to me for help, and instead I had acted unprofessionally and only reinforced his delusions. I had failed him, and I suddenly felt sorry for both of us.

Nicolai began to explain. "I truly communicated with my uncle. There was no sense that he had died. He seemed fully alive, and he spoke to me like a real person. He argued with me, and I found I could not disagree with anything he said. In the end, he persuaded me.

"Somehow, he showed me a complete history of our people in a way that I had never seen before. It became clear to me how difficult it is for my people living in Siberia. I saw how they had lost their religion and power because of the tremendous pressures from the outsiders and evil spirits among us. I saw some of my friends who have taken jobs that required them to become Communists. I saw how their souls had left them, and how they had become tools of evil.

"I journeyed again and again with my people from winter to winter, without hope, without joy, frightened all the time. They were even afraid to pray quietly to their ancestors and protectors, because they could be sent to prison if anyone even guessed they were doing it. Doctor, this vision you enabled me to see has opened up something inside me that has always been closed off. Now it is accessible.

"My uncle left me no choice. He told me I really have to become a shaman. If I don't do this, my sickness will increase terribly. He says I'm the only one who can do this, and that my people's time of lost faith will end. It is toward this goal that I am to work for them. I still don't know what to think about it. I know nothing about being a shaman! But at the same time I feel it is my true way of life. I will need time to understand exactly what I am going to do."

It was strange that I didn't fear his words, for they were very dangerous. In a time only recently past, we could both have been put in prison for them. Even now, with the declaration of perestroika and new thinking, the wrong person hearing his words could still cause much trouble for us.

But I was not afraid. I found that I related to many of the things he was talking about. I didn't know much about the suppression of native peoples, but I knew what it meant to have to hide one's religious beliefs. I had been secretly baptized in the Russian Orthodox Church by my grandmother in Kursk, and I had often been confronted with my inability to express my strong attraction for the teachings of Jesus Christ. My daily life did not offer the possibility of going to church or communicating with holy people. Owning religious or esoteric literature of any kind, including the Bible, was forbidden. If found, such books would threaten the security of one's home in a moment.

As I felt Nicolai's strong feelings, they changed my own. I no longer cared to evaluate my therapeutic abilities in the context of Nicolai's treatment. I felt that something important had happened, and what I wanted most was to understand it.

Nicolai interrupted my thoughts, saying, "I was asked by my uncle to give you a message."

The idea seemed so crazy to me that I did not respond.

"Mamoush said to me, 'Tell this woman that very soon she will meet the Spirit of Death. Tell her not to be frightened.'"

I didn't like these words at all. I had never appreciated predictions of the future, especially dire ones like this. I stared at Nicolai's clothing. His shirt was unbuttoned at the top, and he lacked a tie. It helped me to remember that he was not an oracle but only a factory worker who was the friend of a friend.

My experience told me our session was essentially over, and I also remembered that the newly admitted woman still needed my attention. I decided to wrap up my meeting with Nicolai quickly. "I don't know anything about a message from your uncle, Nicolai, but I want to wish you success in whatever you choose to do. I believe you have the ability to make all the correct choices, but if you need additional help, please feel free to call upon me. Right now, though, I have to see an emergency patient who has just been admitted."

Nicolai also seemed ready to finish. "That's fine, doctor," he replied. "I appreciate your time and your help. Perhaps we will meet again. Good-bye for now."

As soon as he left my office, I quickly crossed the small room to stop the frigid air still pouring in through the open window. For a few quiet moments, I stood and looked down at the grounds below. My session with Nicolai had been unusual and would require time to understand and integrate into my experience. I watched Nicolai as he walked through the hospital grounds toward the bus station. His quick and decisive steps were those of a man certain of his purpose. I closed the window using the same stick with the human head carved by "God."

3

I was responsible for the care of ten patients in the women's ward, and my duties included meeting with each of them every other day. I could never decide whether I preferred working with women or men. The differences were tremendous.

While my male patients were often interesting and a few had even become friends within the boundaries of the doctor-patient relationship, many were criminals whose mental states had to be thoroughly evaluated and summarized in long reports for the court. I never enjoyed the disproportionate amount of bureaucratic paperwork that this required. Even though I realized the necessity of it, I resented the fact that it robbed me of time I would have preferred to have spent with my patients.

Women were simpler procedurally, but my natural inclination to relate and empathize with them as wives and mothers often made it difficult to disassociate enough to maintain my necessary professional detachment. I found that working with women was far more threatening to my inner harmony and required much more emotional balance.

As I entered the women's ward one of my patients called out to me. She had just received a picture of her daughter from the orphanage where her daughter lived, and she wanted me to see how beautiful her little girl was. She had probably been as beautiful once herself, before her disease had begun its destructive path. I thanked her and told her I would have to look more carefully at her picture later, as I was very busy today.

The women stood in line in the ward corridor to get their medication, wearing the dull drab cotton dresses that were handed down patient after patient, year after year. The nurse gave the prescribed pills to each woman, watching to make sure they were all swallowed. Many patients refused to believe they were ill and tried to conceal their medications rather than take them. The nurse couldn't turn her attention away for even a moment. Occasionally she shouted at the women to hurry up, open their mouths wider for her inspection, so she could move on to the next patient.

Some chronic patients lay on their beds in the hallway. It was common for the hospital to be overcrowded like this. As I walked through the corridor, almost everyone wanted to tell me something. I acknowledged each woman but didn't stop to talk, for I didn't have the time. My day was almost finished, and I still didn't know how long it would take to deal with the new patient.

As I neared the emergency room, I heard a scream from the ward where the violent patients were kept. "I know who you are! Nobody knows it except me! But I know who is hiding inside the doctor!"

The screaming girl was still young, but she was already one of our longest-term patients. She had been sick since childhood and had been admitted to the hospital at least twice a year ever since. She had returned again just a few days ago. I hadn't seen her yet because a different doctor was attending her. I had been told she was pregnant again, probably from her unfortunate habit of vagrancy at train stations. The doctor responsible for her had decided to abort her pregnancy without her consent. It was not the first time this had happened in the young woman's pathologically disturbed life. There was no chance that she would ever be capable of raising a child.

In other cases involving mentally ill women who were already mothers, custody of their children was usually transferred to one of the youth care organizations. I had tried to train my emotional being to detach itself whenever this had to be done, but I was not always successful. I often remembered a former patient of mine who had been named Olga, like me. When she was in a normal state of mind, she was a caring and loving mother. She had a soft, beautiful face, and it was always hard to imagine her as the terrible, destructive entity she could transform herself into during one of her psychotic episodes. Her psychosis might well have led her to starve her children or beat them to death, as she listened all the while to the voices that played themselves out in her demented mind.

Both of her children, a four-year-old boy and a nine-year-old girl, had been taken from her by the court, a decision based on a psychiatric commission's conclusion. Afterward, Olga would sit in a corner of the ward's hallway crying silently to herself. I had been one of the commission psychiatrists, and while I was completely comfortable with the necessity of our decision, I couldn't avoid the feeling of guilt I experienced every time I saw Olga crying so desperately in her corner.

I approached the violent patients' ward and looked at the screaming girl through the open top of the dutch door that guarded the entrance. She was standing on the other side of the door, grasping its top edge with her hands. Her short black hair was disheveled. Her big dark eyes shone with a sick light. She had painted her lips and cheeks with bright red lipstick and looked excited and out of control. I had been her doctor a few times in the past, so I knew she was not dangerous. "Katia! I want you to calm down. You don't have to shout here." She immediately became passive, giving me a wry smile as she moved to the corner of the room by her bed. As she reached it, she turned and had the last word.

"Okay, doctor. Let's play hide and seek. But I know who you are."

The new patient I had come to see was in the emergency care room. Three nurses surrounded her bed, making it impossible for me to see her as I entered the room. Intravenous feeders laced above her were already connected to her body.

"How are you, doctor?" a nurse asked as they moved apart, giving me access to my patient.

"Hello. How is she?"

"Doctor, she is dying," said an unfamiliar voice. I turned to see a man rising from a squatting position in the corner of the room. He was tall and thin and obviously had not slept for a few days. His face was pale, with dark yellow patches encircling his eyes. He was clean shaven and wore a business suit, but his neat surface appearance didn't hide the fear and anguish he was feeling.

One of the nurses rushed to explain the situation in whispers. "Excuse us, doctor, for allowing him to be here." There was a rule that relatives were not allowed in the emergency room, and it was seldom broken. "He begged us to stay, and he was in so much distress we were unable to refuse."

"Could you wait in my office, please?" I asked him. His reluctance to leave showed clearly on his troubled face. He was suffering intensely and seemed on the verge of tears.

"Please, doctor," he begged. "Allow me to stay. She is dying. . . ."

"I don't think so, sir. I need to examine your—is she your wife?"

"Yes, she is."

"I need to examine your wife, and then I'll meet with you. Please, wait for me in my office."

I was relieved when he agreed without further argument, and I asked one of the nurses to escort him.

Now I could turn my attention to the woman. My first impression of her was disturbing. She was a mere skeleton covered by slack yellow skin. Her hollow eyes were closed. Her breathing was shallow and fast. A large needle entered her skin near the clavicle, and liquid nutrition fell in slow drops from a bottle above her head, making its way down a transparent tube into her body. This should restore some vitality into her body over the course of the next three or four days. She was motionless, yet I sensed she was conscious and aware of her surroundings.

I came closer and took her hand. It was hot and dry. Her pulse was a bit faster than normal, but otherwise it was strong and rhythmic. I gave her a physical examination. There appeared to be nothing wrong with her except for physical exhaustion from malnutrition. Her organs seemed strong enough to return her to full health with careful treatment.

"I know you can hear me," I told her, touching her hand. "And I'm sure that you will feel much better soon. We'll do our best to help you."

She responded by opening her eyes and looking up at me with shocking hostility. Her eyes were a beautiful deep blue, but they were full of a hatred that distorted her whole face. She didn't say a word. She just looked at me for a long time, transmitting through her eyes a look that seemed to come from another world. It was not a human gaze, but yet another glimpse into the disease that turned my patients from light to dark, from life to nonexistence. I did not want to touch her anymore and withdrew my hand quickly as she closed her eyes.

The medications the doctor on duty had prescribed seemed fine, so I told the nurses they could continue as they were doing.

I shared an office in this ward with another psychiatrist who had already left for the day. His office was bigger and less cozy than my own in the men's ward. My new patient's husband was sitting there when I arrived, looking as if he was in a deep trance. He was staring intently at a picture in a small, dark wooden frame, which he held in his hands in such a way that I was unable to see it.

Seeing his distress, I began the conversation by acknowledging his desperate need to stay at his wife's side. We made arrangements for him to remain with her for the night in the emergency room.

He thanked me and then asked me to look at the picture. He explained, "I would like you to see her picture before the sickness came. I think it may help if I can tell you about my marriage with this woman, whom I love more than anything else in my life."

I took the picture from his hands as he continued to speak rapidly. He talked without stopping in one long, seemingly never-ending breath. He told me about things he probably hadn't ever spoken of before and perhaps hadn't even realized fully himself until then. He babbled on, from one of those extreme emotional states in which the inhibitions of self-reflection and pride have been completely submerged. It was as if he was being carried by an emotional stream into which humans might fall only a few times in their lives.

"You know, my colleagues mostly laugh at me. Crazy wife. Sure. They never ask me about her or say anything insulting, but I always feel their attitudes. My good luck is that I'm an excellent mathematician, so I have status. I'm a chief of a big laboratory, and I love my work. The only two things I have ever cared about in my life are my wife and my work.

"When we were young and she was still healthy, we had a wonderful time together. We called it love, but now I don't remember it as that. I think love is very different from the attraction of youth. The latter disappears so quickly, but love is something we can keep forever. During all these years of her disease I have never spoken to her about this, but I know she didn't love me. In fact, I think she must have come to hate me. She tried again and again to kill herself, every way she could think of.

"Doctors told me that these suicide attempts were the result of voices inside her head that made her do it, but I think it was her own will. I don't understand it. You are the professional. You may have some scientific explanations for me. I just believe that at some point she made a choice against life and that she has tried to follow this choice with invincible strength."

A pretty young blond woman looked out at me from the old photograph. She had an old-fashioned high hairdo and wore a revealing dress with an open bodice showing her beautiful neck. She looked like one of the movie stars of the sixties. The only remote similarity between this woman and the skeleton in the emergency room was the bright blue energy coming from her eyes, although in the picture the cold fury I had seen was lacking.

"Ivan Sergeyevich!" I could not help exclaiming. "Why didn't you come to the hospital earlier? Your wife has eaten nothing for more than a month, yet you did not get help. Why not?"

"It was her wish." He spoke very quietly now. "She didn't allow me to get help. She wanted to die."

"Then why did you finally bring her now? Why didn't you let her die at home?"

"I'm very sorry, doctor. Very sorry. I shouldn't have waited so long, and I understand that her condition is my fault. It has always been difficult for me to go against her will. I'm so sorry." Ivan showed signs of breaking down as he spoke these last words.

I felt bad for making him feel so guilty, especially because I didn't think his procrastination would prove fatal. I was sure that his wife's physical state, if not her mental one, would return to normal quickly.

"Don't worry, Ivan Sergeyevich. I feel certain your wife will recover her health. Fortunately, we have all the necessary medicines in the ward."

He did not even bother to mask the fact that he didn't believe me. He stood up, in a hurry to return to her side, and I let him go to her.

I wrote all the pertinent data of her disease and treatment history in her hospital records. It had been a long, hard day, and I was looking forward to going home. As I left the ward, I saw Ivan through the open door of the emergency room. He was so focused upon his wife that he didn't notice me at all. I saw him turn her body over and wipe her back with a cotton swab dabbed in alcohol, to prevent bedsores. He knew how to take care of her, which would be a big help to our orderlies while she was here.

As always, my way home offered a pleasant contrast with my morning ride. The hospital was almost the first stop, so the nearly empty bus gave me my choice of seats. As it so often did, the restful trip through the countryside at the end of my long workday rocked me quickly to sleep.

Soon I retraced my morning steps to my little studio apartment, and then I cooked and ate a simple dinner of fried potatoes and a fillet of Ob River fish, sold to me in the open market by some of the same fishermen who accompanied me every morning in the bus. I would have enjoyed some greens with my fish and potatoes, but they were not available in winter.

After my meager meal, I went to bed and fell asleep quickly. In the middle of the night, I suddenly awakened in panic from a nightmare so strong it felt more real than my waking moments. The dream was so persistent that it followed me even after I sat up in bed and turned on the light. I could still hear the cold, remote voice of the unknown Mongolian-looking man who had appeared to me.

Again and again he repeats, "I want you to see her journey!" This makes no sense to me at all, but that doesn't stop him. Then the energy shifts. I see a woman, my new emergency patient, Ivan's wife. Her beautiful white shape forms an extreme contrast to the frightening, dark, empty space in which she floats. She moves slowly and gracefully, flying higher and higher. Gradually she turns toward me. Her face is beautiful again. Her body is normal and healthy, with an alive, womanly shape that shows no signs of her sickness.

I try to escape this vision, but the movie reel of the dream continues. The mysterious Mongolian-looking man controls the scene, which becomes more terrifying with each moment. Now the woman looks directly at me, her eyes victorious and taunting. Her gaze hypnotizes me. It feels as if she is stealing my will.

"She is a rare, powerful woman," the man says in a hoarse voice. "She did everything she was meant to do simply and quickly. She did

what everybody else here does, but she is more honest and brave than most."

I watch as the woman moves into a kneeling position, facing a large white figure that has suddenly appeared above her. Her face becomes ecstatic and trancelike. She now looks very much like the picture from her youth. The white figure slowly cascades down over her, entirely covering her now prostrate body.

The feeling created by reexperiencing this vision was so intense it began to break the dream's hold over me. As quickly as I could, I tried to put myself fully beyond it. To awaken myself fully and recover ownership of my being, I lectured myself that this had been just a dream, and that the woman I had seen in it was actually sleeping soundly in her hospital bed, where I had left her. I told myself I was simply too tired these days and that I must do something about it soon.

These artificial attempts to reassure myself didn't fully erase my fears. I couldn't dismiss the mixed feelings of attraction and fear that had entered me upon seeing the powerful image of the immense, flowing white figure that had covered and engulfed my patient.

It was hopeless to try to sleep again after the dream. I could barely wait for dawn to arrive, and I caught the first bus to work in the morning. I was anxious to be busy again, hoping to loosen the strong hooks the dream had plunged into my consciousness. I tried not to think about it on the way to the hospital, concentrating instead on walking the steps into the ward again and again in my mind. The ward would be a safe haven where my nightmare would finally dissolve and I could return to normal again, free of anxiety.

At last my actual steps reached the ward door. I turned at the top of the stairs, opened the door, and entered. The first few breaths of air with its familiar odor of urine mixed with sweat and medicine were almost welcome today, as a reminder of my regular reality. Now I would be with other people. I would be forced to use my mind. I would be the doctor, the psychiatrist, the one who is in control and out of reach of strange voices and images in the night.

It was so early when I arrived that my patients were still asleep in their rooms and the blue night light in the corridor was still on. Everything was calm and peaceful, almost surreal after my agitated state. I saw that the door to the emergency room was closed. Perhaps poor Ivan had been able to nap during the night.

Walking among my sleeping patients, their faces distorted by their diseases even in their dreams, I felt a great relief. I was back in my familiar ward. Everything was normal and under control.

The duty nurse was sitting in her office, writing in her journal. I wondered how I would explain my early arrival to her. Then she looked up, and I saw at once that she was frightened and upset.

"Oh, doctor! Why did they disturb you? She went so unexpectedly and so quickly! Her body is already in the hospital morgue. I told them not to call you until morning. There is nothing you can do now that you couldn't have done later. Oh, doctor, I am so sorry you were disturbed."

I ran to the emergency room and burst through the door. Facing me was an empty bed with crumpled sheets. The room was still in disarray from the night staff's frantic attempts to hold onto a life that had wanted only to move on. The resuscitation apparatus, used syringes, empty droppers were strewn around the room. Machines and modern medicine had been unequal to the mysteries of death, and they had lost the contest.

I squeezed the side of the metal bed in anguish as the nurse entered behind me. "It was absolutely unexpected. Arrhythmia at first; then very quickly her heart stopped. We tried everything, but it was useless. It makes no sense to me at all, doctor."

My body was drained of energy, and I simply nodded my head mindlessly to acknowledge the nurse's words. What I really wanted was to be left alone for a little while, to sort out my thoughts. I left the emergency room and walked slowly to my office, seeing and hearing little of what was around me. My steps were automatic, the footsteps of someone who had traced the same path thousands of times before.

As I entered my office, a nurse asked in her friendliest voice, "Doctor, would you like some coffee?"

"Yes, please." A vase with seven white roses was standing on my desk. It was unusual to see such beautiful flowers in the wintertime. They seemed misplaced in the stark surroundings of my office.

"I added a little sugar to the water to keep the flowers fresh longer," said the nurse as she brought me the coffee. "They are from Ivan Sergeyevich. He went to a funeral parlor and came back with these flowers. He specifically asked me to give them to you. Can you imagine how he found them in the middle of winter?"

I understood that the roses were Ivan's way of telling me he didn't blame me for his wife's death, yet I still felt profoundly shocked by what had happened. It had only been a day since my strange meeting with Nicolai. Now I found myself faced not only with the completely unexpected death of Ivan Sergeyevich's wife, but also with the added dimension of my mysterious and frightening dream about it. The woman's autopsy report arrived a few days later, but it settled nothing. It showed no reason for her death, leaving me both relieved and dismayed.

It was several weeks before these events began to fade in my memory. In the meantime, I filled my life with the usual routines that can so conveniently help us forget our doubts and traumas. I sensed that my past experiences in the physical world—my training, my rational mind—might not be all there was to life. Something new was present, but I couldn't begin to name it. It intrigued me, and I liked it. I could not contemplate it rationally, so I simply allowed it to exist and tried to carry on with my life as normally as possible.

4

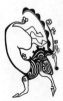

One day a few weeks later, Anna called and invited me to visit her that evening. Even though we usually got together at least twice a week, I had never brought up Nicolai. She had mentioned once that he seemed to be doing all right, and that he was very grateful to me for my help.

Anna and I met right after work and sat, as usual, on the old narrow couch in her one-room apartment. I was browsing through the latest issue of a movie magazine, reading about new films and wondering if we should go out tonight instead of just staying in and talking. Anna was smoking too much and seemed to be nervous. I sensed something was bothering her. I had known for the past few months that she had been having physical problems. Her menstrual cycle had been painful and irregular, coming several times a month, and it was exhausting her. At first it hadn't seemed to be a serious disorder, and I had felt sure she would be treated quickly for it. We were both from families of medical doctors, and I knew her parents had arranged for her to consult with the best professionals in the city.

Finally, she looked directly at me and told me that the doctors still hadn't been able to diagnose what was wrong with her. They told her that even more tests would have to be done and that they couldn't begin any treatment at all until they knew exactly what her problem was.

In the meantime, her condition was visibly becoming worse. She looked pale and sometimes almost haggard, because she was paying no attention to her appearance. Her short hair was uncombed, her light blue eyes were not highlighted with her usual carefully applied makeup, and her skin was neither clean nor healthy looking. Even in the few days since I had last seen her, she had deteriorated. She talked about how very tired she was and how difficult it was just to get up in the morning to go to work.

I couldn't imagine Anna waiting much longer for definitive treatment, so I suggested she do something quickly. My advice was to go to the hospital where, along with professional observation, she would also get a good rest.

Anna agreed she needed to do something right away, but she didn't want to go to the hospital. Instead, she asked, "Do you remember Nicolai, the man whom you saw as a favor to me?"

I nodded my head. Of course I remembered him.

She continued, "You probably remember he is my neighbor. Well, I met him yesterday on the stairs. He asked how I felt, and I told him everything. I was very depressed about my illness, and I guess he sensed it. He is leaving soon to return to his village in Altai, and he invited me to go with him. He suggested I seek a healing from one of the elders. It will probably be in April, a few weeks from now, when the worst part of winter will have passed.

"Somebody from Altai has told him about a woman healer. People say she can heal anyone. I am losing faith in my own doctors, and I can't help wondering if this woman might be able to help me. Nicolai told me she has cured mental patients as well, so I thought you might be interested. Perhaps we could go together. Will you come? It would comfort me greatly."

I looked at her in surprise as she spoke, growing more astonished with each sentence. Going to Altai seemed crazy. Anyway, I was planning to spend my vacation in the summer, in the warmth of the sun on the Black Sea, not in April in a remote Siberian village that would probably still be buried in snow and ice. I told Anna I could not possibly go but that perhaps she should. At best, the woman might help her. At worst, it would get her out of the city on a journey with a friend.

But as our conversation turned to other things, I found that the idea would not leave me alone. I felt a subtle longing in my deepest self to meet this woman who healed people. The more I tried not to think about it, the more strongly the idea had me in its grasp. A silent voice in the core of my being told me that this invitation to Altai could be a doorway to an understanding of the strange, unexplained events I had recently experienced. Something unknown seemed to be rising to the surface of my life, and I felt more and more that I must allow it to happen.

It seemed more than a coincidence when a few weeks later, during the hospital staff's traditional early morning tea, several of my colleagues commented that I had been working too hard, that I looked much too pale, and that it would probably do me some good to get a short rest by taking part of my vacation right away. With relief and a sense of excitement, I found my decision to visit Altai was made. I called Anna immediately to let her know I would be joining her.

She was delighted and rambled on about the details of the trip. "But you know, we are leaving tomorrow. I don't know if you will be able to get tickets for the same train. Why don't you take any train you can get to Biisk, and just let me know the train's number. We will find you at the station and travel the rest of the way together.

"I am so glad you decided to go, Olga," she continued. "Today I started to think it was wrong for me to do this, but now I feel it is the only thing for me. I don't have any idea what kind of healing I will go through, and I'll feel much more at ease with you along. Thank you. We'll see you in Biisk."

I got a ticket on the number eight train and telephoned Anna to tell her. My train was to arrive two hours later than the one she and

Nicolai were taking, but she said they would be happy to wait. Nicolai had arranged for a neighbor from his village to pick us up by car at the train station. Since there was no public or commercial transportation to Shuranak, Nicolai's village, the only way to get there was by private car.

I packed a small suitcase with a minimum amount of clothing and went to the train station by taxi. The number eight train left Novosibirsk at ten P.M. and arrived in Biisk the next morning. As I walked toward the station and the waiting rail car, I couldn't help but notice that even this late in the evening, the feeling of spring was all around me. Spring was in the steps of the people in the street and in the sound of birds singing mingled with the tinkling of melting snow falling as water. The dark air was fresher, and gone was the cold knife of winter that cuts through all but the warmest clothes.

As usual, the station was filled beyond its capacity. There were not enough chairs for even one-third of the passengers and visitors. Parents and their children were sleeping on newspapers on the floor and on the wide inner ledges of closed windows. Small children carried by their mothers were crying, yet less desperately than usual, as if they knew that the seasons were changing and the warmth of summer would soon return. Even inside the stuffy station hall, with people sitting and sleeping everywhere, there was a pleasant air of anticipation.

My train was on schedule, which was a relief. It was just as dirty and stuffy as I expected, and I felt fortunate at having to spend only one night on it. From the conversation of my neighbors in the small compartment, I gathered they were a coal miner's family. The husband was taciturn, the wife tired but generous, offering me a piece of their fried chicken although they barely had enough for themselves. Their two-year-old boy was already asleep when they got on the train and, amazingly enough, did not awaken even with the commotion of all the other passengers climbing aboard.

I politely refused the chicken and offered them my lower bunk to sleep on. I climbed into the top bunk, pleased to be where I would not have to answer any questions about where I was going, who I was going to see, or how long I would be there. The woman had obviously been eager for conversation, but I was not. With the first rhythmic sounds and movements of the train, I fell immediately asleep. I knew that tomorrow I would find myself in a new world.

The sounds of metal spoons clinking against glass awakened me the next morning. The family members were drinking their tea after having finished off yesterday's chicken. The train had almost reached Biisk, which delighted me. I had time only to wash my face quickly in the one small bathroom in the car, after first standing in a long line with the many others who had come to do the same.

The train had already entered the outskirts of the city by the time I was able to sit down and look out the window, so I had not yet seen what kind of country we were in. Knowing that Biisk was at high altitude, I expected at least to see mountains in the distance. Instead I saw only dull gray blocks of apartments that all looked exactly alike, surrounded by a few scraggly trees. The scene outside looked so much like Novosibirsk that it was not inspiring at all.

The train made one last strong jerk and then came to a full stop at the station. Passengers were looking out the windows, craning their necks, searching for those who had come to meet them. I found myself doing the same thing. To my disappointment, no one on the platform looked familiar.

I took my suitcase down from the luggage rack and said good-bye to my night neighbors. As I departed, the strong upland air quickly confirmed my expectation that spring had not yet arrived in Biisk. Some of the smaller trees were still almost completely covered with deep snow, and the early morning atmosphere was absolutely frigid. Before I even had time to finish my thought, my skin was already tingling unpleasantly with the extreme cold.

A drowsy porter appeared behind a huge handcart that rumbled loudly as he pushed it along. He was wearing an apron that at one time had probably been white but over time had become so dingy that it de-fied description and could no longer be called any particular color at all. He asked if he could carry my tiny suitcase to the taxi area.

I barely had time to say no before I heard Anna calling my name. She was laughing excitedly as she ran toward me from the opposite side of the platform. "You gave us the wrong car number, and we were waiting at the other end of the train. I'm so glad you made it!" she said, hugging me.

Turning toward the exit, I noticed Nicolai standing quietly close by. He greeted me informally this time, as a friend rather than a doctor, and he looked very different—more cheerful, more relaxed, and more assured of himself. He even looked older. His black hair had grown since I last saw him. He had pulled it back in a ponytail, and he was wearing warm work clothes.

I greeted him as he took my suitcase from my hand, and we walked toward the street. The only vehicles parked outside were two old taxis, a few private passenger cars, and a khaki-colored jeep. The driver of the jeep got out and walked toward us. He was a tall, strong-looking man wearing dirty knee-high rubber boots, a warm overcoat, and a black rabbit skin cap with earflaps.

Nicolai introduced him to us as his neighbor, Sergey. Sergey promptly made it clear he was not happy to be there and had come only from a sense of duty. His impatience to get back to his village showed in his gruffly barked orders to get into the jeep.

Anna and I obediently sat as we were directed to, in the back seat. Anna whispered to me that from his authoritarian manner, Sergey had probably just gotten out of the army.

"He is too old for the army," I replied, both of us giggling. The jeep's engine sounded terrible, but it seemed to run well enough, so we began the final leg of our trip to Shuranak. No one was out walking at this early hour, but many cars were already on the city streets. Most were old, dented automobiles whose engines made even louder noises than ours. Occasionally a big truck would pass dangerously near us, leaving behind a dirty brown cloud of exhaust that hung undiffused for a long time in the frozen morning air.

Finally we left the city without seeing anything different from the small glimpses I had already caught of it from the train. If there was anything special about Biisk, I had not seen it. We were soon on the main highway, accompanied only by a few transport trucks. The less frequent the buildings became, the more trees we saw. Soon the trees hugged the road, getting bigger and bolder and seeming to close in on the narrow highway as we sped along.

Sergey was so good at avoiding the awful potholes in the road that I quickly forgave him his curt army manners. He and Nicolai sat in the front seats, gossiping about local village news. Anna and I filled the time talking about some of our mutual friends. Gradually the hypnotic rhythm of the road quieted all of us, and we lapsed into a natural silence.

It took more than three hours to get to Shuranak. It didn't seem that long, for my attention had become absorbed by the scenery outside our speeding jeep. I found myself in a kind of trance. The melted snow at the road edges became whiter and whiter the farther we drove, and the giant evergreen trees seemed to merge into each other from the windows of the moving jeep.

Having lived for so long in a busy industrial city, I had forgotten what it meant to be with nature. Even my few visits to country houses from time to time had been devoted to socializing, and there had been no room in these short visits to experience the beauty of the natural setting. Now the forest we drove through completely commanded my attention. I sensed a tremendous power in its mighty trees with their old, gnarled trunks, in the deep black-green of the evergreens, and in the rhythmic movements of the trees, which suggested their oneness with the wind.

We navigated a turn in the road, and suddenly the first panoramic view of the Altai Mountains reached out to us. The gentle ridges of these ancient mountains, with the rays of the sun lighting their rounded peaks from above, created exquisite patterns of lights and shadows. This soft beauty held so gently within the ruggedness of the mountains was something I had never seen before, and it literally took my breath away.

The road became narrower and more winding. The countryside looked so primordial that it was difficult to imagine human life sustaining itself here. But when the first small houses of the village finally appeared, they seemed wholly natural in their setting. We passed a few old wooden houses placed far enough away from one another to seem somewhat remote and isolated, yet close enough to remain connected to the common energy of the village. An old woman near one of these houses had come out to do something in her still snow covered garden. She straightened up attentively as we passed and looked sternly at our jeep. Finally we stopped near a small green house tucked behind a wooden fence.

5

"Here we are," said Nicolai, opening the jeep's passenger-side door.
The bark of what sounded like a very large dog came from somewhere
inside the high fence. The upper half of a doorway was visible above
the fence. It opened, and we heard a woman's voice calling, "I'm coming! I'm coming!"

As we got out of the jeep we continued to hear her voice, now yelling
at the dog to be quiet and get out of her way.

We took out our baggage and stood patiently near the fence. "It's so
beautiful here," Anna said, taking a deep breath. I nodded my head
silently. As I did so, my eyes and other senses reminded me that somewhere in my past I had experienced another strange, wild place like
this, although I could not remember where or when.

Finally the fence gate opened boldly, revealing a small, middle-
aged woman with a fur coat thrown over her shoulders. Her beautiful,
moonlike Altai face was lighted by warmth and kindness. It was Nicolai's mother, Maria, and she quickly escorted us out of the cold and
into her home.

We drank tea around an old dark wooden table and settled in. After
a few hours, we were becoming quite comfortable in our new surroundings. Anna and I were at once tired and excited, our minds natu-

rally wandering to thoughts of the next few days. Nicolai was obviously relaxed in his mother's home. He understood the major, life-changing commitment he had made in returning to his village, and he was clearly content with it.

Finally, darkness began to gather around the small village. Maria waited until twilight to turn the house lights on. Later we learned that she was beginning to worry but trying not to show it. The message Nicolai had sent through a neighbor had said only that he was coming home with two friends, both of whom were medical doctors. Maria had expected two people who fitted her experience with doctors—middle-aged men wearing suits and glasses. She had worried the whole day about how she would meet these serious, intellectual friends of her son's and had even prepared a few questions to ask them. Now two young women were sitting at her table instead, and they presented an entirely different dilemma.

If we stayed in the house with her and Nicolai, it would supply gossip for the whole village for months to come. She could already hear the talk. "Why would Nicolai bring not one, but two girls to his home village? And how could Maria, his mother, allow them to all stay together?"

Even if the neighbors' gossip had not been an issue, the two-room house was so small that even fitting four people into it was a real problem all by itself. She slowly drank her tea, outwardly trying to look calm, while on the inside her mind was churning. How could she deal with this surprise her son had presented? She fervently prayed to herself, "O great Ulgen's daughter! You who are wise and full of kindness, help me! Give me a sign of what I should do." She hoped for an answer, but none came.

Unaware of Maria's dilemma, Anna and I were becoming more and more fidgety in our need for rest. Maria was equally anxious and was irritated at Nicolai, who seemed completely oblivious to the awkwardness he had created.

While Maria sat thinking, her attention suddenly fell on the tambourine hanging to the right of her front doorway. She had made this small tambourine after her brother Mamoush's death, at the advice of some village elders. They had told her that she must do this because her brother was a kam—a shaman—and the tambourine would help him to remain here on earth. It was beautifully made, and she was proud of it, even without fully understanding its purpose. Now the tambourine reminded her of her brother and gave her the solution she was so desperately seeking. The girls could stay at Mamoush's house. "Of course!" she said to herself. "How could I not have thought of this earlier?"

She suggested this to Nicolai as she slowly sipped her tea. My mind was wandering, and I only half heard her words. "It is okay," I said, realizing that some decision was being made about our lodging and that I might be able to close my eyes shortly. "We can stay wherever is most convenient for you."

"As long as it's not outside," teased a tired Anna.

Nicolai sat deep in thought for a few minutes before answering. Then he agreed and asked his mother for some bed sheets. We thanked her and ventured into the night, our destination a dead shaman's house.

The sky was bright, with thousands of stars and a half moon overhead. The cries of the night birds coming from the forest might have been frightening somewhere else, but here they seemed natural. Fears found in the night can only live close to their sources. Giant cities, with all the tensions and aggressions of too many people placed too close to each other, were much scarier than the night sounds of the forest around this tiny village.

A man and two tired women walked slowly on the snow-surrounded path, intermittently talking and laughing, making their way toward one of the most remote houses in the village. Mamoush had purposefully placed his house on the far north side of the village, at the top of a hill.

Nicolai lit a candle as we entered the house, for there was no electricity. Everything inside was covered by a heavy layer of dust, but the air was fresh. The house was no more than one elongated room with a single window in the left corner, near an old, narrow bed made from dark wood. On the other side of the room was a small kitchen area with a fireplace. A huge bear's hide covered the middle of the floor. An old pair of men's boots made from reindeer hide stood almost directly on the bear's head. At first taken by surprise by the little house's strangeness, we gradually warmed to it.

"Olga, look at me!" Anna exclaimed. She had discovered a strange assortment of feathers that had been made into a hat and had put it on her head in a moment of silliness born from feeling tired and a little bit nervous. Now she looked comically at me from underneath it.

"Is it me? Does it fit?" she asked. The hat had been made from an owl. The upper part of it was the bird's whole head and body, with open eyes, beak, and ears. Its wings had been pulled down and made into side flaps that now framed Anna's face.

"It is not you at all," Nicolai said. He took it off Anna's head and placed it on the opposite side of the room.

Anna, who had quickly inventoried the room, asked to sleep in the narrow bed, leaving the bearskin on the floor as the only other possible bed for me. Nicolai made up both the bed and the bearskin with sheets and blankets and then disappeared to walk the lonely path back to his mother's house. Anna and I wasted no time in blowing out the candle and falling into our beds. It had been such a long and interesting day.

I almost collapsed onto the bearskin, greatly appreciating having any place to lie down at all. It took only a few minutes to discover that the goose-down blanket was not going to be warm enough by itself, so I placed my own fur coat over the blanket and snuggled into my unlikely bed.

I could tell by Anna's deep breathing that she was already asleep, but I was finding it hard to relax. The transition from my usual comfortable world to this bearskin bed in a dead shaman's house had been so fast that I hadn't realized how overwhelmed I felt until I lay down. Now the slight scent of the bearskin, which had not been too noticeable at first, became more and more disturbing, creating an uneasy feeling in my mind. There were none of the familiar sounds of my home to calm and quiet me. There was no familiar clock's ticking, barely heard at the side of my bed; no neighbors' voices wafting in through the thin walls of my apartment; no traffic sounds outside. I hadn't realized before that some of the things that bothered me about my little city apartment had also comforted me and had become a part of my conditioning for sleep.

The bright light of the moon coming through the single window illuminated the few objects around me in the nearly empty room. A vertical stack of wood for the fireplace stood like a sentinel at the door. To my right there was an old white chair, into which Nicolai had thrown the owl hat. The hat seemed to come alive as I stared at it in the semidarkness. Above me, near the window, was a small table. From where I lay on the floor, I couldn't see what was on it.

On my left, an old oval hand drum made from animal hide was leaning against the white wall. Its face was turned to the wall, and I could see only the open underside. Its handle was made from two carved pieces of wood, crossed at right angles to each other and joined in the middle. The wooden cross pieces had been carved into the symbolic figure of a man. The longer piece formed his body, with the head supporting the top rim of the drum and his feet pressed against the bottom. The other piece had been shaped into the man's hands and arms, with nine metal rings through the fingers of each hand. The drum was big, almost three feet across the oval's longest dimension. In the middle of its skin surface, visible even from inside, was what appeared to be an intentionally cut slit. I imagined how loud this instrument must have sounded before it was broken. As I imagined its rhythm, the drum appeared to draw near me, closer and closer, until its dark form seemed to fill my entire vision and I was not sure if I was awake or dreaming.

I must have fallen asleep immediately and slept very deeply. Later, I remembered a strange dream. In it, I had stood next to a heavy wooden door that shone brightly with polish. The door was closed. I reached out to touch it, and as I felt my hand upon it, my hand became more and more real to me. The more I moved it, the more fully aware I became of myself and all my other senses.

I realized I was still sleeping and inside a dream, yet at the same time I had conscious awareness and complete freedom of will. I knew I had the power to use my hand to open the door and enter the space behind it. There was a sweet sense of joy in my heart, and I wanted the dream to continue. Then there was a sudden realization that somebody else was in my dream, waiting in the space behind the closed door, and that this person could see me with the same level of consciousness as my own. This scared me. I stopped moving my hand and everything dissolved.

We woke up at dawn to the total silence of the peaceful village. The morning sun shone brightly through our one small window. Even in the light, the dead shaman's strange house didn't lose its frightening atmosphere. It made me remember the story Nicolai had told in the hospital about his uncle dying, here in this very house. Obviously a place like this could induce deep psychic distress in people who were naturally inclined toward such things. Nicolai belonged to this group. Standing in the shaman's house, waiting for Nicolai to come and take us from it as soon as possible, I understood his story much more clearly.

Fortunately, Nicolai arrived soon after we got up and invited us for breakfast at his mother's house. Before leaving, I asked him about the drum. It impressed me even more in the early morning light than it had in the darkness. Even broken, it seemed strong, powerful, and alive.

"It was my uncle's drum. I only saw him use it once. After his death, a few of our old people came. They told my mother the things that must be done after a shaman's death. One of them was to break his drum. It is an unwritten law. They told her that the drum should serve only one shaman. The spirit of the drum must be sent away after the shaman's death through an opening made by a relative. So my mother did it.

"Today we are going to see Umai, the shaman of Kubia, a nearby village. She will know much more about this rite of passage, if you want to ask her."

We were glad to leave Mamoush's house, which still seemed threatening even in the light of day. Maria's friendly little place, busy with the breakfast preparations, made a reassuring contrast. Maria was cooking eggs, warming black bread, and pouring real milk with a top layer of cream, making a hearty morning meal to prepare us for our day's journey.

We had no idea what was planned for the day. When we asked Nicolai how we would get to Kubia or how far away it was, he silently ignored our questions. He told us only to dress in the warmest clothes we had brought and to follow him. Maria gave us a packet of bread and cheese to take with us.

6

If I had known how cold and difficult the journey to Umai's village would be, I would not have come. We walked endlessly through deep snow on a small mountain road, really no more than a narrow path that sometimes almost disappeared in the snow. My Italian leather boots were not made for this, and before long my feet were soaked.

After an hour, Nicolai still had told us nothing, and we began to wonder if we would be able to complete the journey. At first we tried to laugh about it, but soon the cold and altitude affected us and we became exhausted. The beauty of our surroundings no longer cheered our spirits at all. We began to speculate, only half joking, about dying here on this rugged mountain path, wondering if our bodies would even be recovered. The fact that our deaths might not even be noticed amidst the tranquillity of this snow-covered mountain road surrounded by huge evergreen trees was a sobering thought, one that helped us keep walking, step after painful step.

It was Anna who first noticed smoke rising above a small house. She joyously jumped as high as she could and then hugged and kissed me in her excitement.

Nicolai confirmed to us this was Kubia, and we were glad his irritating silence had finally ended. As we neared the village, Anna and I were happy to think that we would soon be in a house again, sitting before a warm fire, no longer having to walk through the endless cold snow. However, I had noticed that Nicolai had begun to seem nervous.

"I need to tell you something," he finally said. "I need to warn you that I don't know exactly how the people here will react to you."

We just stared at him, at a loss for words.

"We are here to see Umai, who is a kam. We don't use the word *shaman* ourselves. That is not our word. *Shaman* is a word created by the Russians. We call such people kams. The problem is that you are Russians. Our people have a good relationship with white people, but it is superficial. Maybe no one in Kubia will explain anything to you about the kams or their rites and rituals. And it is even more likely that no one will allow you to see what actually happens at their healings. I didn't know this before we came. My mother only told me this morning. She said there could be a problem for you in meeting Umai."

It sounded stupid and absurd that after all the effort we had made to get to this forbidding place, Anna might not be allowed the healing she had come for. I started to laugh, but Anna became furious. "It's not funny, it's crazy," she said. "I am seriously ill, and I have come with Olga to this forgotten, out-of-the-way place in hope of help. It was you, Nicolai, who invited us here. It was you who brought us on this long, cold, dangerous journey today. And now you tell us that we could be thrown out of the village? To do what? Die in the snow?"

"Why did you do this?" I asked him incredulously. "Are all of your people as irresponsible as you are?"

Without hesitation, Nicolai replied, "My uncle, Mamoush, told me to bring you with me." As he said the words, his nervousness subsided and he looked more calm and sure of himself.

"Excellent!" mocked Anna. "Here I am in the middle of frozen nowhere with a mental patient, and a friend who is supposed to be a psychiatrist. Olga, did you not examine Nicolai at the hospital?" She looked at me accusingly. "Even I, who am not a psychiatrist, could tell you he has obvious symptoms of mental disease."

I felt bad that Anna had said this and even worse as I realized her words had some truth in them. Nicolai stood near us in silence, and I felt sorry for his embarrassment. Finally I spoke. "Anna, we are already here. We have committed ourselves. To go back now is not a possibility, as we need to rest first. We have no choice but to enter the village." I felt a little calmer and hoped my words would also help Anna relax.

"Let me tell you something," Nicolai said. "Things happened here almost a hundred years ago that greatly affected our people's attitude toward strangers. People who were foreign to us and our land decided to bring their own religion here. One day they called the kams from near and far for a ritual. They told them they wanted peace between their religions. About thirty kams came, bringing only their drums. The strangers took all the kams and put them into a small wooden house. Then they covered the house with kerosene and lit a match.

"The house with the kams in it burned for hours. None of the villagers could do anything. When it had burned to the ground, three of the kams got up and walked out of the ashes alive. The strangers were terrified by this. They did not try to stop the three kams but ran from the burned house and watched in shock as the kams walked away. The three kams went in different directions and continued "kamlanie." But from that time on, the kams have performed their rituals in secret. Umai is a descendant of one of the three kams who walked from the fire.

"Were the strangers Christians?" asked Anna.

"No," Nicolai replied. "We had Christians later, and then the Communists came."

Without any further words, we moved toward the waiting village.

I saw Anna gently touch Nicolai's hand and heard her ask, "Will you forgive me?" I knew she spoke of the words she had said in anger a few minutes before. He nodded and released her hand quickly.

The village was similar to Nicolai's, but the houses were smaller and the people seemed even poorer here. We approached one old house with smoke rising from its ancient chimney. There were no people on the streets, no barking dogs to announce our presence.

"I believe she is here," said Nicolai, as we stopped near the door. "You had better wait for me," he added as he pushed the unlocked door open and disappeared into the small confines of the house.

My wet feet were becoming frozen. Anna took a cigarette out of her pocket and smoked. We waited nervously for what seemed a very long time. Finally Nicolai emerged from the house and walked directly up to Anna.

"Umai will heal you this night." His words seemed to hang in the air for a moment until our worried ears fully understood them. "She told me to take you to another house, where you will wait for her. She said she has felt your wish to heal your body and return to your normal life." He took Anna by the hand and led her toward a house on the other side of the street.

"Wait, Nicolai. What about me?" I shouted.

"Umai told me to ask you why you came here. Wait here for me. I'll be right back."

I was stunned and confused. This simple question surely shouldn't have troubled me, yet it did. Why was I here? This must all be a strange dream. Traveling here, I had felt vaguely as if I was moving toward some kind of mystical experience, but at no place along the journey had I tried to consider a rational explanation. I could say I had come as a tourist, simply joining my friend to see the mountains. But that was not true, and I knew it would not be an acceptable answer for the woman inside the house. Once again I was facing the consequences of not making conscious decisions with my life, and I felt sorry for myself.

When Nicolai returned and touched my hand, he startled me. I told him the first thing that entered my mind. "I came here to learn from her."

He went into the house again. Almost immediately he reemerged and gestured for me to enter. Coming in from such a bright day, I thought at first the house was entirely dark. As my eyes adjusted, I realized that a small amount of light entered from two tiny windows. I saw that the house had only one large room and looked absolutely empty, except for two women. "Hello" was already out of my mouth before Nicolai quickly gestured to me to be silent and to sit down on the floor in one of the corners.

One of the women was lying face down on the floor in the middle of the room. Her back was naked, with traces of dirt and herbs on it. The other woman looked older. She was short, with a strong, healthy body. Her clothes were strange to me: a long skirt made from heavy winter fabrics of different colors, with a few small cloth dolls sewn on its back. She had dark hair, mostly covered by a blue shawl, and a Mongolian face aged with many wrinkles. I would have guessed her age at about seventy.

She didn't seem to notice me. She looked very busy and was concentrating on carefully placing a strange object near the woman lying down. It was a crude triangle made from three pieces of wood, each about three feet in length. The recently cut wood still had the fresh color and even the aromatic scent of the pine tree it had been made from. Images of fish were carved all over the flat surfaces of its sides.

I realized that it must be Umai standing over the other woman and that a healing was taking place. Umai placed the triangle with the fish on the right side of the other woman so that it separated the two of them from a big deer hide that lay on the other side of the triangle.

Nicolai was sitting in the far corner of the room, so the whole space around the two women in the middle was open. Umai took a small drum from the floor and started beating it softly. At first her rhythm was broken and weak, sounding uncertain. Then she started to sing in her native language. The words of her song had a pleading intonation as she moved gracefully around the motionless body below her.

The woman on the floor made no sounds and appeared to be sleeping. Her back was naked except for the dirt and herbs. Although the temperature inside the house was only a few degrees warmer than outside, her body looked relaxed and warm. Umai walked around her, sometimes bending over and beating her drum right above the woman's back. The rhythm of her song became clearer, the words louder. She moved faster and faster.

Watching the swift energy of her dance, I now thought she must be younger than I had first guessed. The power of the drum increased so much that it seemed impossible for such a small instrument to sound so loud. Umai's voice took on an incredibly deep, forceful tone. I hardly recognized her as the same person I had seen begin the dance. She looked taller, stronger, more aggressive and masculine, almost like a warrior in a duel to the death with a powerful enemy. She jumped and spun her body with unbelievable quickness and strength. Her song transformed into a battle cry. She breathed deeply and quickly, her eyes lit with a victorious glow. Then she took the woman harshly by the shoulders and screamed to her in the Altai language.

The woman rose to her knees. Her hair hung down in tangles. Her eyes were still closed, and she appeared to be in a deep trance. She crawled on her knees to the wooden triangle. The opening in the triangle was the exact size for a human to crawl through, and she entered it.

Umai screamed even more loudly at her. She threw the drum away and pushed the woman deeper and deeper into the triangle with her bare hands. Her screams changed into a plaintive chanting. It was difficult for the woman to pass through the triangle. Her bare body convulsed and wiggled as it scraped painfully against the rough ends of freshly sawed wood. Umai tried to make it even more painful for her by moving the triangle back and forth, scratching the woman's body continuously as she slowly pushed her through.

I had become totally absorbed by what was happening. Suddenly the fish carved on the wood became alive to me, swimming from left to right along the triangle's sides. Umai continued to chant as the woman neared the end of her struggle to pass through the triangle. When she was almost completely on the other side, Umai jumped over to her and lifted the deer hide. The woman crawled underneath it and soon was totally covered.

Umai then became even more furiously aggressive. Screaming, threatening in her gestures, she picked up the wooden triangle and destroyed it. She did it with a look of intense hatred, as if legions of her enemies hid within it. She trampled it down and then beat it with her hands. It sounded as if she was cursing it crudely in her own language. When only the remains of the shape lay on the floor, she did the same with her drum. Soon there were only pieces of wood lying scattered around the woman, who still lay covered by the deer hide.

Umai turned toward Nicolai and said a short phrase in their language. Somehow, I understood that it meant he should help the woman under the hide. Umai again appeared to be just a small, elderly native woman, but I knew now that she had a tremendous power within her. She sat down on the floor, took a pipe from a hidden pocket in her dress, and started to smoke. She watched Nicolai calmly as he helped the woman get up and put on the rest of her clothes.

The woman looked tired and sleepy. She didn't seem to notice Umai at all and moved slowly toward the door with heavy steps. She opened it and went out without a single word or gesture. This surprised and impressed me. I had expected her to show gratitude, to tell Umai how she felt—anything but show such complete indifference toward her healer.

I turned to look at Umai, trying to read in her face any reaction to the way the woman had left. Unexpectedly, I discovered her staring at me with an intense and tricky gaze. She said some words to Nicolai and continued staring at me, still smoking her pipe. I couldn't take my own eyes away from her, and I found myself smiling stupidly into her face.

Nicolai translated her words for me. "She said you did well in helping her make the fish take the spirit of the woman's disease and carry it down to the lower world."

Umai stood up and rearranged the remains of her healing session on the floor. Then she walked over to where Nicolai was sitting and had a short conversation with him in their native tongue. I knew that even if she spoke Russian, I wouldn't hear any words of it from her.

Nicolai turned toward me. "She wants you to follow her to another house in the village, where she is staying. She doesn't live in this village, you know. No one knows where she lives. This house we are in now was deserted when the family living in it moved to the city a few years ago. It is a place where Umai comes only to heal people."

I asked if we were going to where Anna was waiting for us, hoping I would be allowed to watch and perhaps even help in my friend's healing. Nicolai answered that he had no idea where Umai was going to take me.

While we spoke, Umai had moved to the door and opened it. I discovered that I hadn't noticed the passage of time, for daylight was almost gone and the street was already in muted darkness. Umai motioned me to the door, and I moved out into the twilight after her. She was still wearing only her dress, with no heavy coat to protect her from the bitter cold. She walked quickly down the frozen street, turning in the opposite direction from the house where Anna was waiting.

I heard Nicolai say, "I'll go to Anna."

I followed Umai's figure down the narrow path of packed-down snow between high walls of snow on either side. Lamplight gleamed from some of the windows as we passed, looking cozy and warm from where we walked in the cold night air.

Everything I had experienced during the day had stretched my consciousness so much that my mind was quite unsettled. I wasn't tired, neither was I frightened anymore. Although I had no idea what to expect next or what Umai might want of me, I decided to let go thinking about it. For the second time in two days I vaguely recognized my feelings as an echo from another time, but I still couldn't remember where or when it had been.

7

Finally, we came to a large house with two doors, one on each side. The left half of the house had a light on, and I could see people moving about inside. Umai walked to the other door, on the right, and easily pushed it open.

The room behind it was almost perfectly round, without furniture except for a single sleeping pad covered with an old blanket. It was dark, and something in the way it felt awakened a strong premonition of danger in me. I would have felt even more uneasy except for the reassurance of Umai's calm face. Somehow, without understanding why, I already felt as if I knew Umai well. Perhaps it was because her face reminded me a bit of my grandmother's, which had features that recalled many Russians' Mongolian heritage. I followed Umai's face constantly, trying to keep eye contact with her every second. Without this, I felt my fear would rise up and I would be lost.

She turned on the light and motioned for me to lie down on the sleeping pad. I lifted up the old blanket sewn from pieces of different colored fabrics and began taking off my coat. She made signs for me to stop, so I lay down under the blanket in all my winter clothes. The floor was dirt, not much warmer than the outside, and I immediately felt the cold creeping up from below. I wondered how long I would be lying there.

From where I lay, I watched Umai as she built a fire in the middle of the room and then turned off the light. There was no firepit or fireplace, just a fire on the dirt floor in the middle of the empty room. The flames shooting up looked quite mysterious. Though I had never seen anything like this before, there was a strange familiarity to it that made me long for some old, unknown, forgotten time. Umai sang softly in words I could not understand but that seemed to be addressed to the fire with love and devotion.

Although I had been among the people of Altai only a short time, I had an intuitive sense that they were mainly centered in the present. They did not live in the past. They did not dream of the future. Umai was focused completely in "now," and at this moment "now" meant making a fire.

As the flame illuminated the room, my fragile calm disappeared and danger again seemed to lurk all around me. I could no longer see Umai's eyes, because she refused to look at me. She took something from her pocket and put it into the fire. The flame swallowed its new food like a hungry animal, grew higher for a few seconds, and then returned to normal.

Umai's song changed, and I began to feel as if I was somehow inside it. Something was happening within me. My attention was captivated by the smoke rising from the fire. I could not look away, nor could I think of anything else.

Splintered thoughts come racing through my head with incredible speed. Only two have time to register in my mind: "I am very cold" and "This is psychosis." The second one makes me panic. The feeling that I am losing my world floods through me. Using all my strength, I try to find that place inside myself from which I can speak. I don't know how to speak. I have lost my voice. What does it mean to say "my"?

Suddenly a voice emerges, sounding far away. It is shouting something. Losing my sense of self, I surrender, having no idea of what or who remains here. I become the voice, the shouted voice high above that rises up with the smoke of a fire in the middle of a room in a forgotten village in Siberia. My last efforts to bring my world together become a transformation, an integration of the smoke and the voice into one. And now the voice and the fire are me, and I am a snake rising up through deep, resistant water.

Simultaneously, another fear embraces me. I am underwater, swimming as fast and as hard as I can to get to the surface. Nothing surrounds me but water, deep water. Faster and faster I swim, trying desperately to reach the surface.

Finally, the moment comes when I break out of the water and float on the surface of the ocean. Instantly it becomes a place of peace and calm. I love this ocean and could float like this in it forever. Nothing disturbs me. There are no thoughts other than an appreciation for this water that now holds me up. I begin swimming. I swim and swim until I see the coastline. I realize that land meets this mysterious body of water on all sides and that I'm swimming in a big round lake. Now I notice what is on the coast. It looks like a city. I can see buildings, cars, and people. Panic takes me again. This is my city, my friends and my relatives. I don't want to go back to them. I want to perceive nothing but the soft, flowing water.

A soft, feminine voice comes through my panic. "Be calm. I will talk to you now." It is Umai's voice. I don't know what language she speaks, but I know it is Umai and somehow I understand her words.

"Now you are in your inner space, the place of the Spirit Lake. This is your first conscious time here. Each of us has this inner space, but during the lives of most people, it becomes smaller and smaller. As we go through life, the world around us tries to fill up and kill this inner space, your Spirit Lake. Many people lose it entirely. Their space is occupied by legions of foreign soldiers, and it dies.

"Now you have experienced this space within yourself. Now you know it. You will no longer be afraid of the world around you. Your *space will never be filled up with anything but yourself, because now that you have experienced it, you recognize its feeling and its pulse. You will continue to explore it. Later you will also learn that there is an important Inner Being who lives there. You will need to meet and understand this Spirit Being. I will help you do this when you are ready."*

Umai's voice is soothing, and I hang onto every word as she continues. *"This next thing is the greatest secret I could tell you. We have the task of building two things while we are in our physical lives. Our first task is to construct the physical reality in which we live. The second task is the creation of ourselves—of that very self that lives within this outer reality.*

"Both tasks require equal attention. Keeping the balance between them is a very sacred and demanding art. As soon as we forget one task, the other can capture us and make us its slave forever. This is why the place of the Spirit Lake, the home of the Inner Being, becomes empty and dead for so many people. They come to truly believe that the outer world is the only one worth their attention. Sooner or later they will realize their mistake.

"For you, the main danger is not this but only in exploring your inner self. This is why you were already so interested in other people's minds. You were using that information to try to understand your own psyche. You must learn how to accept the importance of creating your own reality. Believe me that your work with the outer world has an absolute and equal power and ability to satisfy. Don't be afraid of the shore around you now. Everything you see there is your own manifestation, and it is ridiculous to be afraid of your own creation. I will help you."

The environment around me starts to disappear. Vision and awareness begin to return to my physical body, and I remember that I am this body lying on the ground. I want to sleep, and I am almost there when Umai's old hands give me a cup of hot herb tea with

milk. I sip the hot liquid slowly before succumbing to the heat of the
warm tea and falling asleep.

The morning light was the next thing to touch my consciousness. As I awakened, I realized I was still on the floor covered with my winter coat and the old blanket, alone in the strange room. It took all my strength to remember what had happened the day before. Everything had a dreamlike quality, and I knew I was hanging precariously between two worlds. I needed to see another human to help prove to myself that I was still alive and sane.

I could hear two men's voices behind the thin wall separating my room from the other side of the house, but the voices were too muffled for me to distinguish what they were saying. Getting up was tricky, and I stood shakily for a few seconds while my legs got used to the idea of supporting my body again. There was no water to wash my face, no mirror, no makeup.

I thought of how I must look and of how ill prepared Anna and I had been to start on such a journey. I remembered the cheese and bread Maria had thoughtfully given us the day before, and hunger enveloped me. I decided to find Anna and to have breakfast with her and Nicolai as soon as possible.

My wool shawl was terribly crumpled after spending the night sleeping in it, but I was glad I had the extra warmth it provided. My boots were standing near the mattress, and someone had thoughtfully put warm wool socks on my feet.

8

After making my makeshift bed and putting on my boots, I stepped out into the bright day. The air was so incredibly fresh that the first breath made me feel calm and happy again. The blue sky was layered in fluffy white clouds, birds were singing from the tall evergreen trees that surrounded me, and the distant mountains looked like a beautiful postcard picture. Everything seemed to carry the message that life could still be harmonic in some places on this earth. I was glad that fate had given me the opportunity to visit one of them.

"Hi!" called a man's voice from the house's other doorstep.

"Hello!" I responded, listening to see if my voice had been changed by all the experiences of yesterday and last night.

"My name is Victor." He spoke Russian without an accent, marking him as another visitor to the village, like me. "The owner of the house told us that an old woman would be staying here last night and asked us not to be surprised by anything that happened. But are you this same woman who is supposed to be so old and scary? We didn't know we would have such attractive company next door!"

"Almost," I replied. "My name is Olga."

Something in his words, his facial expression, and his tone of voice made me cautious. For all its beauty, Siberia was still a very isolated place. Strangers were a rarity, and unattached female strangers even more so. A lone woman without a husband or family to depend on could be vulnerable, and care was sometimes necessary to avoid creating awkward or even dangerous situations.

Fortunately, my psychiatric experience had many useful aspects. Being young and working mainly in the men's ward, I had quickly learned from necessity how to transform male interest into friendship without romantic or sexual overtones. Instinctively, I felt that this rough-hewn outdoorsman, with his large, muscular body and deep, masculine laugh, would find the topic of intimate bodily functions embarrassing enough to submerge any other notions he might have.

"I'm afraid I really need to find a bathroom right away," I said. "Is there a toilet here that I could use?"

He gestured toward a small narrow cabin in back of the main house, and I quickly made my way there. Victor was waiting for my return with a friendly, protective look on his face. He introduced his friend, Igor, who was standing beside him. Igor was the complete opposite of Victor, short and thin, with sharp facial features. They invited me in for breakfast and a cup of morning tea, and the prospect of food was much too good to pass up.

As I entered, I couldn't help but be surprised at the totally different environment that greeted me. Their part of the house looked like a normal home. It was warm and tasteful, filled with many beautiful handmade things. The table was covered by a white tablecloth hand embroidered with flowers. A big copper samovar sat on top of it. Translucent cotton curtains allowed light to pass through the small windows, and there were real porcelain cups to drink from, with old Russian designs. Everything here made me feel at home, and I found myself relaxing a little.

"Are you two the creators of all this beauty? It is hard to imagine how two mountaineers like you could put all this together so exquisitely," I teased them.

"Are you the witch we were told about yesterday?" they laughed back. "Seriously, only these things are ours," Igor added, pointing to a corner where I had already seen their large mound of mountain-climbing equipment. "We just rent this place as a base for our trips into the mountains."

The tea they made was very hot and probably as strong as anyone could have made it. And they had one of my favorite jams, oblepiha berry, which they served on hard little biscuits like brittle crackers. After the startling experiences of the day before, it felt good just to relax and exchange some lighthearted banter. I knew that I had been given too much to integrate in a short time and that thinking about it wouldn't particularly help right now.

Oblepiha berries grow on trees found only in Siberia and are the source of many legends I had heard over and over again as a child. Oblepiha was used for everything from treating a small cut on a child's hand to a miracle cure for cancer, and it contained vitamins beyond counting. I loved it especially because of its unique, bright orange color. Every autumn our family would go to our country house to pick these berries.

We had to be very gentle while picking them, making sure we didn't destroy the thin delicate skin that would break so easily in our hands, allowing the sweet, sticky, orange juice to explore every crevice in our fingers. They weren't easy to pick, because the leaves were quite thorny. My fingers always ended up decorated with dots of blood, with small bits of broken thorns embedded in my flesh. Trying to come away from the harvest with my fingers thornless and reasonably free of the sticky orange juice was an exercise I never forgot.

I realized that my new acquaintances had been talking and joking with each other while I was daydreaming, and I pulled myself back to the present. They didn't seem to have noticed my brief distraction and continued telling me their stories of mountain climbing. As I listened, it occurred to me that they were so dedicated to their sport that they probably had few conversations that didn't quickly turn to their experiences in the mountains. In a short time, I was told in detail of all the big and little differences between the mountains of the Caucasus and central Asia, and I relived with them all their most difficult times there. With enthusiasm to match their detail, they told me of their friends who had died on mountain peaks and passes. And of course they spoke a lot about their beloved Altai Mountains.

However, even in this comfortable haven with two eager conversationalists, I still felt emotionally distant. Some other time I might have been more enraptured by their storytelling, but now I found my mind constantly wandering back to my experiences of the day before. The only time their verbal meanderings through the mountains caught my full attention was when they mentioned Belovodia. I had heard many legends about this place. Belovodia, which means the land of white water, was said to be a mystical, hidden country that had been found and entered only by a chosen few. It was believed by many to be somewhere in the Altai Mountains. Some people believed that Belovodia was another name for Shambhala, a sacred country spoken of in many Indian and Tibetan myths, from which the holy people were said to have governed the world.

"Did you know that even the Dalai Lama recently said he believed Shambhala to be somewhere in Altai?" asked Victor.

"I know nothing about the location of Shambhala," said Igor, "but I'm sure Belovodia is in the Altai Mountains. I've climbed many peaks on this earth, but nowhere else have I seen such white rivers. Scientists would probably explain the color as coming from some strange mixture of the soil here, but nevertheless, I believe it is because of Belovodia. Furthermore, if I were a spirit governing the world, I would choose to do so from Altai. It is the only place from which the rest of the earth could be governed, if you ask me."

Victor added his own thoughts. "You know, tremendous fissures have opened up in the ground throughout Altai, uncovering layers millions of years old. Some say radiation from the earth comes to the surface and dissipates from these fissures, covering the whole of Altai like an umbrella. That is probably why Altai is so unlike anywhere else, and why even old materialist Leninists like us feel that miracles are possible here."

"Could you tell me more about this mysterious country?" I asked. Victor's words about Belovodia had touched me deeply.

Igor spoke again. "No one from outside knows much about it. The native peoples have ancient stories about meeting spirits and mysterious priests from this hidden country. We have never met any ourselves, but we believe it is possible."

"Do Altai people call them shamans?" I asked, thinking of Nicolai and my recent conversation with him.

"We have never been told anything about such things from the Altai people. You could ask them yourself. I don't think shamans still exist. But who knows?" The subject of shamans obviously did not interest Victor, and he dismissed the subject quickly.

"If you are interested in knowing more about this elusive subject, here is something you can read. The owner of the house gave it to me," said Igor, handing me a brochure of about fifteen pages with *Belovodia* printed in large letters on its cover.

As they continued talking, I opened the brochure and began to read.

In 987, the Grand Duke Vladimir Red Sun in Kiev was looking for a new religion for Rus, his country. He sent six separate ambassadors, each bearing great riches, to faraway lands. Their instructions were to learn and bring back the beliefs of these lands, in order that Red Sun might choose the best of them.

Soon afterward, a wandering holy man visited him. The Grand Duke shared with the wanderer a dream that had been coming to him night after night, month after month. In it, an old man spoke to him, saying that a seventh expedition should be sent forth, but the man in the dream didn't say where to send it. So the duke asked the wanderer to go out into the world and to find out in seven days where the seventh ambassador should go.

The holy man went into deep meditation and fasted. On the seventh day, the priest from the last monastery he had visited in Greece came to him in a dream. He reminded the holy wanderer of the ancient story of Belovodia, a remarkable country of eternal beauty and wisdom in the East. Only those who were called upon—a few specially selected persons—would be allowed to find and visit it.

The wanderer told this story to the Grand Duke, who became excited. He decided to send an expedition to the East, led by the wanderer, Sergey, to find this mysterious country. Six men of noble families, as well as many servants and porters, were given to Sergey as helpers. The number of people who went on this pilgrimage was three hundred and thirty-three. They were instructed to return with their news in three years.

The first year, many messages arrived at the Grand Duke's palace amidst great cheer and hope. The second year nothing was heard. The third year, as well, nothing. Seven, ten, twelve years passed with no more news from the expedition. At first, people had scanned the horizon for them, eager for the good news that surely would accompany them. Then the people became fearful that the worst had happened, and they stopped watching for them. Many prayed and regretted the search for Belovodia. After twenty-eight years had passed, people began to forget that the expedition had even taken place at all. Then time covered everything.

Forty-nine years went by, and finally an old monk arrived in Kiev from Konstantinopol. Later, feeling that his life was nearing its end, the old man decided to tell his secret. It could only be passed verbally from monk to monk, as it was sacred knowledge. He said this secret would eventually become the possession of all the people on earth, but only when the time was right. At that time, a new era would begin.

He told the following: "I am that same Father Sergey who, fifty-six years ago, was sent by the Grand Duke Vladimir Red Sun to look for Belovodia. The first year was calm and safe. We passed over many lands and two seas. The second year led us through the desert and it became harder to continue. Many people and animals died. The roads became impassable. We couldn't find answers to our questions, and our people became more and more dissatisfied.

"The farther we traveled, the more we found the bones of both people and animals. Finally, we reached a place completely covered by bones, and the people refused to continue. We made a joint decision that only two men would continue with me. All the others would return home. At the end of the third year, my two comrades got sick and had to be left in a village along the way.

"As I traveled on alone, I found guides in a few other villages who told me that from time to time wanderers had passed through their land searching for a mystical country. Some called it the Closed Country. Others called it the Country of White Water and High Mountains or the Country of Light Spirits or the Country of Alive Fire or the Country of Alive Gods. The legends of Belovodia had, indeed, traveled far and wide.

"Finally, one of my guides told me that from where we stood, the mysterious country could be reached in three days. My guide could take me only to the boundary. After that I must travel alone, because the guide would die if he crossed into the mysterious country. So we proceeded.

"The road going up the mountain was so narrow that we had to walk in single file. High mountains with snow-covered tops were all around us. After the third night, the guide said I had to continue alone. In three to seven days of walking toward the highest point in the mountains, if I was one of the chosen few, a village would appear to me. If not, I would not wish to know of my fate. The guide left me. I watched as his returning steps dissolved into nothingness.

"The rising sun lit the white mountaintops until they seemed as the roaring flames of a fire. I was the only being in sight. I was alone with my God, who had brought me here after such a very long journey. A feeling of indescribable, unearthly exultation filled my being. I knew I was embraced by a spirit. I lay down on the path and kissed the stony soil, my heart and mind quietly thanking God for his grace. Then I went farther.

"Soon there was a crossroads. Both paths seemed to lead to the highest part of the mountains. I chose the right one, which went toward the shining sun. With prayer and song I continued to walk. There were two more crossroads on that first day. At the first of them, one of the paths was blocked by a moving snake, as if it closed the way for me, so I took the other path. At the second, three stones blocked one of the paths. I took the path that was clear.

"On the second day, there was one crossroads. This time, my path divided into three parts. Above one of them a butterfly was flying, and I chose that one. After midday the path led alongside a mountain lake.

"On the third day, the rays of the rising sun lit the white, snow-covered peak of the highest mountain and surrounded it with flames of fire. My soul burst forth in awe at the sight. I looked and looked at it. It became a part of me. My soul joined with the flames around the mountain, and the fire became alive. There were white figures turning, flying toward the top in streams of flame in beautiful circle dances. Then the sun rose up from behind the mountain, and this mesmerizing vision disappeared.

"There were three crossroads on the third day. The first had beside it a beautiful, bubbling, emerald-hued creek with white froth dancing over a myriad of stones and moss. I quickly chose the creek path.

"About noon I reached the next crossroads. Three paths branched off from it. One went near a cliff shaped like a giant idol protecting the way. Without thinking, I took that path. At the next crossroads, which also had three paths leading in three different directions, I chose the path best lit by the sun's rays.

"As darkness descended on this third day, I heard strange sounds. Soon, on the side of a hill, I saw a dwelling lit by the last rays of the sun. I arrived at this small dwelling before dark, entered this humble refuge, and gratefully fell asleep.

"In the morning I was awakened by voices. Two men were standing in front of me, speaking in an unfamiliar language. Strangely, my inner self somehow understood them, and they understood me as well. They asked if I needed food.

"I replied, 'Yes, I do, but only for my spirit.'

"I followed them to a village where I stayed for some time. There I was told about many things and given some duties and work to do. I felt tremendously contented. Then one day I was told the time had come for me to travel farther on my journey.

"I was treated as a beloved relative when I reached the next new place and then again was taken farther when the right time had come.

"I lost count of time, because I had no way to think of it. Every day brought something new, something surprisingly wise and wonderful to me. Time passed as though I were in a miraculous dream of all good things. Finally, I was told that it was time for me to return home, which I did.

"Now that I am about to leave this world, I am telling you what it is possible for me to tell. I have held many things back because your human mind could not accept everything I saw and was told about.

"The country of Belovodia is not a fantasy. It is a reality. It has been given many different names in the folk legends of the people. The Great Holy Beings, the facilitators of the High World, live there. They work together constantly with all the heavenly Light Powers to help and guide all peoples of the earth. Theirs is a kingdom of Pure Spirit, with wonderful flames, full of charming mysteries, joy, light, love, inspiration, ease, and unimaginable greatness.

"For each one hundred years, only seven people from all over the world are allowed to penetrate this country. Six of them return with the sacred knowledge, as I did, and the other one remains.

"In Belovodia, people live as long as they want. Time stops for anyone entering within the kingdom. They see and hear everything that goes on in the outside world. Nothing is hidden from those in Belovodia.

"As my spirit grew stronger, I was given the opportunity to see beyond my body, to visit different cities and to know and hear everything I wished. I was told about the fate of our people and our country. There is a great future for us."

I slowly turned the pages of the brochure, marveling at this bizarre yet strangely believable tale. At the end of the brochure was a notation that the text had been written down in 1893, penned exactly as the words tumbled out of the mouth of a dying monk in a monastery. I was amazed, as I realized that this story had been passed down orally from 987, when the Grand Duke first sent his ambassador out into the world, until 1893, when it had finally been written down.

I felt a strange excitement, realizing that I held this small book in my hands almost a hundred years after it had been written. Turning it over, I could find no sign of an author or publisher. I asked my new friends about it, but they could tell me nothing more.

"The only thing I could add to it," said Victor, "is that one of my friends, a professional photographer, used to come here once in a while to take pictures. He was so impressed with Altai that he decided to live here. He is convinced that Belovodia is here, and he has his own extensive theories about it. He has seen some deep, rocky crevices in the mountains with only ice beneath them. He told me that when the sun lights these places, fire is visible. This sight is so unlike anything else he has ever seen that he is sure it is the location of Belovodia."

Victor looked at his watch, and I saw it was approaching noon. I was surprised at how much time had passed and began to worry about Anna and Nicolai. I quickly said thanks and good-bye and departed into the bright light of day to find the house into which Anna had disappeared the day before.

9

The only street in the village looked more real and normal in the morning than it had the previous evening. As I walked along it, I recalled my night's experiences and the feel of Umai's presence. It was easier now for me to think of it all as a dream. I had no context for Umai in my morning state of mind. I couldn't even imagine her being in the village.

One thing about yesterday's experience had bothered me more than anything else. My seeing a vision could be explained using different psychiatric tools, but I had no idea how to rationalize the fact that I had seen carved fish swimming up pieces of wood and then later been thanked by Umai for helping her make them become alive and swim away with the disease. How did she know I had seen them moving? Was it just a coincidence? Not having an answer to this destroyed the rational explanations I had for everything else that had happened.

This question was too disturbing for any more thought. To quiet my mind, I just concentrated on my steps as I moved toward the house in which I had left Anna. I hoped that being with Anna and Nicolai would help me bring some order to my thoughts and emotions and allow me to fit together the elusive pieces of this strange puzzle.

Cautiously, I approached the door to the house and knocked a few times, each knock bolder and louder than the one before. No voice answered, nor was there any sound of steps moving toward the door. Finally, I pushed the door and it opened. The window shutters were tightly closed, and the house was in darkness. At first I couldn't see anything, and I thought the house might be empty. When my eyes got used to the darkness and I could see the dim outlines of some pieces of furniture in the room, I entered.

Searching for Anna, I moved slowly from the first room to the second. Still I saw no one. I thought that perhaps Anna and Nicolai had gone out to look for me and that we had missed each other. My thinking was so confused that I momentarily forgot it would have been impossible for us to miss each other, there being only the one road through this tiny mountain village.

A slight sound on my right made me turn toward the wall. I looked frantically for the light switch, and when I finally found it, I was confronted with an image of Anna that I will never forget. Her figure was slumped awkwardly against the wall. She was motionless and gave no indication she was aware of my presence. Her hands had been tied with a thick dark cord that looped through two large metal rings attached to the wall. She was half sitting, wearing only her underwear, her head slumped forward toward her chest. Her hands were open and I could see they were covered with small cuts and dried blood. I thought my friend had died.

"Anna!" I screamed in terror. She made a slight movement, and a soft groan escaped her lips. I sat down beside her, holding her shoulders, trying not to give way to my emotions. She slowly opened her eyes and looked at me. Ugly, dark patches under her eyes made her face look old and haggard.

"Help me, Olga," she said in a tired, weak voice.

Coming out of my initial shock, I began to work with the thick cord, freeing her hands as quickly as I could. I was afraid to ask Anna what had happened and instead concentrated on untying the cords to release her. Then I helped her across the room and made her comfortable on a big bed that was in the opposite corner. Fear and confusion overtook me, and I found myself crying, sensing that something irreversible had happened to her.

Hearing my sobs, Anna spoke. "Stop crying, please. Nothing dangerous happened to me, Olga. I just didn't sleep enough."

She gestured toward her dress, which was draped across a chair. I helped her put it on, her mind still not totally present and her body still recovering.

"Right, Anna," I replied. "And because you couldn't sleep, you tied your hands to the metal rings on the wall. Then when you still couldn't get to sleep, you cut them with a knife. Look at you!"

My emotional outburst made me feel better. Anna appeared to be gaining strength, her body moving more easily now, and she looked at least a little like her old self. I watched her carefully and was relieved to conclude that nothing serious had happened to her.

"But, Olga, it was my own decision to do this. I didn't know exactly what to expect, but Umai did tell me it might be difficult. She asked if I was ready to suffer a little in order to drive away my disease, and I readily agreed. So it was my decision. I'll be all right. Just give me some time." Her voice weakened again, but she showed no other signs of abuse.

Finally, with a deep sigh, she began to describe the events of the previous night. After we had parted yesterday, Nicolai had brought her to this house and had left her alone to wait for Umai. She had waited a long time, but fortunately she had found an interesting novel and had spent the time reading. Finally, Umai had arrived and wasted no time beginning the healing process.

"The first thing Umai did was to ask, as I told you a minute ago, whether I was ready to suffer. I said yes."

"Wait a minute, Anna. How did you understand her?" I asked, confused.

"Her question was simple enough, and I understood it literally, Olga. She asked me if I agreed to suffer and I said yes. I didn't come all this way to be healed, bringing you along as well, only to refuse because of a little discomfort."

I realized she did not understand my question. "That is not what I meant, Anna. How did you understand her language?"

"What do you mean, Olga?" She frowned and shook her head side to side as if my question made no sense. "Umai may speak with an accent, but otherwise her Russian is fluent."

I wondered if Anna was somehow confused or if Umai did in fact speak Russian. If she did, I wondered, why had she not spoken it to me?

"What she did next," continued Anna, "was to pick up two glass bottles from the table. I believe they were filled with vodka, or at least that was what was written on the labels. She drank both of them quite easily, as though they were water. I can't imagine that they were really vodka, because I don't think anyone could have drunk them that quickly if they were.

"Anyway—whatever was in the bottles—soon after that she did begin to look drunk. She got these cords you saw from somewhere on the other side of the room. Then she asked me to take my clothes off and stand near the wall. It never occurred to me that she might tie me up to it. I walked to the wall, and when I turned around to face her, she was already binding my hands. I didn't have time to think about what was happening to me.

"I guess I accepted everything as a kind of ethnographic game at first. When I realized that she looked very drunk and that she could not or would not answer any of my questions, then I began to feel afraid. I shouted at her, demanding that she answer. I asked her what she was doing. There was still no reaction from her at all, no matter what I did. She just danced around the room, taking quick little steps and singing her monotone song as she moved. She was drunk, crazy, and frightening, and I was completely in her power.

"Being totally helpless like that was the most awful thing I think I've ever experienced. The loss of my free will was terrifying. I think that hell must feel something like that.

"Then Umai began to sing very loudly. She looked completely out of control and not responsible for her actions. Finally I got tired of shouting at her, and since nothing awful had actually happened, my fear passed a little. I decided just to wait patiently for the end of her performance. Then she left the room and returned with a big sharp knife. She came toward me with a menacing air, shouting something in her own language, and began plunging the knife into the wall all around my body.

"Can you imagine how horrified I was, Olga? I thought I was going to die right then. I don't think anybody could imagine how I felt at that moment. I cried. I prayed. I struggled to untie myself, but I was helpless. Then she became even more crazy and started cutting my hands with her knife.

"When I saw the first blood flowing from my body, my fright somehow turned into anger. I was furious at Umai and screamed that I would kill her! She looked at me, and then all of a sudden she completely transformed herself. With a fully sober gaze, she said in Russian that she wouldn't stop until I had driven away my disease. Then she went back into her drunkenness and began pricking at me again with her knife.

"I experienced an incredible feeling of hate, not just in my mind but in my entire body. But this time it was not hatred for Umai so much as for myself, for the situation I had put myself in, for allowing myself to be at Umai's mercy in such a helpless way. This hate flooded up from my feet to the top of my head. I didn't know what to do with the sensation of it. I thought I was going crazy. Then suddenly an animal scream came from my throat. I felt like the animal. I even saw a giant figure of some kind come out of my mouth along with the scream. And then everything changed. I think it was the scream that changed things. My hate dissolved immediately.

"At the same time, Umai became quite calm again and seemed tired. She sat down on the chair in front of me and started smoking her pipe. I felt no more anger toward her at all. I was too exhausted. I asked her to give me a smoke, and she held her pipe to my lips for a few moments. The tobacco was strong and had a scent like none I have ever known. I was still tied up, and I was so very tired.

"'I won't untie you,' she said. 'If I do, you will think that everything was just a dream. You will need a witness. Your bonds will serve this purpose. And don't feel sorry for yourself. Feeling sorry will accomplish nothing. Your friend will come soon. She will help you, and she will be good at feeling sorry for you.'

"With those last words, she laughed and left the house. I fell asleep, right where I was tied to the wall. Then you came and woke me. And you know, she was right. You really were very good at crying over me." Anna finished her story, laughing softly at me.

As Anna talked, I felt more and more as though it had been me who had just been through the terrifying ordeal she described. Everything she said sounded so real. I wanted to ask her more questions, but I saw she didn't have the strength to say more. I was tired, too, so I asked only one simple last question before letting her fall asleep. "Where is Nicolai?"

"I don't know. The last time I saw him was yesterday, when he walked with me to this house. I thought you and he were somewhere together."

"No, we also parted yesterday, and he said he was coming back here to wait with you. Didn't he come?"

"No, Olga. I don't remember seeing him." She was asleep as the last word left her mouth.

I sat back and closed my own eyes for a moment. Thoughts came quickly into my mind. Obviously, the situation had exceeded my ability to handle it. The same sort of thing had sometimes happened before, when I had been in extreme situations in the past. My conscious mind would feel overwhelmed and go numb, while my unconscious would try to choose the best path to take. But this time no ideas at all appeared from my stupor. I was unable to make myself react rationally, and I didn't know whether to cry, run, scream, or just go to sleep like Anna. Everything was happening far too quickly.

I don't know how long I sat beside Anna as she slept, but finally I decided to go back to see Victor and Igor again. These men seemed my only connection with normalcy. They were now symbols of stability and order for me. Once I thought about seeing them, I couldn't move quickly enough. I wrapped my coat around my shoulders, left the house, and walked swiftly down the now familiar road to their house.

I knocked on their door and opened it without waiting for a reply. The tradition of open doors in this village quickly vanished for me, as a stern looking old woman looked up at me, obviously irritated at my intrusion.

"What do you need?" she asked in Russian, in a loud voice vacant of even the remotest trace of hospitality.

"I came to ask Victor and Igor some questions," I blurted out, surprised at having walked in on this grouchy woman.

"There are no such people here," she snapped back at me.

"But I met them here this morning," I insisted. "I stayed here myself last night, in the other half of the house. Umai brought me here."

I was more and more confused and needed to confirm some sort of reality for myself. It was important for this woman to verify that I had been there with Victor and Igor and that my experience with them had been real.

She repeated her words even more curtly than before. "There have never been any such people here. I don't have any idea what you are talking about, young woman."

"Please. Listen to me. Two friends and I came here from Novosibirsk. I am looking for the man from Altai who brought us here from his village. His name is Nicolai, and we arrived here just yesterday. We can't find our way back to his village without him. Can you help me find him, please?"

Instead of softening as I had hoped, the look on her face became even more stern. If it was possible, her voice was also harsher when she spoke. "When I was a young woman I never would have let myself get into such a situation with a man. This is your problem. I know nothing that can help you. Now please leave my home."

I was certain that she knew about Victor and Igor and probably about Umai and Nicolai as well. It was impossible to live in such a small village and not know everything that went on, especially about people who stayed overnight in your own house. But her hostility toward me as a young, unmarried woman from the outside world, traveling with an unmarried man, was all too clear. I knew she had spoken her last words to me.

Feeling angry, I walked back into the street. The street was completely empty. Fear and loneliness were overwhelming me, and, to make it worse, I could sense from the tingling of my skin that people were sitting in their houses all around me, knowing everything that had happened but not willing to help me at all.

"SHOP." The simple sign on top of a house roof caught my eye. I wondered how I could have walked down this street and not noticed it before. Although I was afraid my extreme uneasiness might intensify inside the store, since the door was open I walked in without thinking.

An old Altai man was sitting behind the counter. He was half asleep, nodding his head as his breath wheezed in and out. He wore the traditional, warm Altai robe belted around his huge belly. He was wearing a typical Russian hat, made from dyed rabbit fur, and it obviously helped him feel comfortable in his unheated store. He seemed to notice me only when I rather nervously asked what I could buy to eat. There was no food or drink anywhere that I could see, just a few items for children and things like soap and toothpaste.

Coming slowly to attention, the old man looked at me and said, "Well, you can buy bread and candies. All the rest of the foods I carry

are already sold. I don't know when they will bring more for me to sell."
He looked at me indifferently, but I had the feeling that he knew
everything about me. An intense feeling of tension spread throughout
my abdomen and chest.

I forced myself to recall the cases of railway paranoia, described by
a famous nineteenth-century Russian psychiatrist as a kind of situa-
tional disorder for people traveling by train for the first time. This syndrome was related to many kinds of paranoia caused by unknown
situations. I did not have any desire to experience this psychosis first-
hand, so I concentrated on deciding what to buy.

This calmed me, and I was able to buy some bread and a packet of
dried candies without any further alarm. I had left my purse and all my
documents in my suitcase in Maria's house, but fortunately I found
enough money in my coat pocket to pay for the food. It made me feel
stupid and irresponsible to think how carelessly I had planned and
carried out this journey.

When I returned to the house, Anna was still sleeping. There was
still no sign at all of Nicolai. It disturbed me not to know where he was
or when he might show up.

I realized, too, that something unusual had happened to my sense of
time. It seemed that only a few hours had passed since I had awakened
this morning, but when I looked outside I saw that daylight was already
waning and evening was upon us. I couldn't find my watch and couldn't
remember whether I'd had it with me yesterday or not. I had never felt
this strange compression of time before, and it further confused me.

I felt that perhaps I could ground myself and become more whole
again by concentrating on my physical body. I looked through Anna's
bag and found the bread and cheese Maria had given us yesterday.
Had it really been just yesterday?

While I was putting together a small meal for myself, I heard Anna's
voice from the other room. At first I felt bad that I had made too much
noise and had awakened her so soon. But when she entered the kitchen,
I could barely believe my eyes. She looked years younger, and the happy

expression on her face was like that of a newborn child. She was laughing from some centered place inside herself, and it was obvious she had incredible energy surging through her.

"Hi! I'm back," she said at last, with a youthful grin on her face.

"So I see." I searched her face, first in disbelief, then in great relief that my friend did, indeed, seem to be fully back. And in the process, she looked better than I had seen her look in a long time.

"Olga! I can't believe how wonderful I am feeling. I don't remember ever feeling so healthy and strong. There obviously must be times when one has to experience sickness in order to realize health, and I've done it. Your Umai is a crazy old woman, but I think she can really make miracles."

"I am glad to hear all this, Anna, but she is not 'my' Umai. She is at least as much yours as mine. Especially since I don't understand at all the experience I had with her. If it was a healing, it certainly had enough craziness in it. I felt nearly insane myself after she worked with me!

"Anna, do you have any idea what we should do next? We don't know where Nicolai is, when he will appear, or even if he will appear at all. It is time for us to go home, don't you think? But we don't know how to get out of here by ourselves. Do you have any suggestions?"

"I don't care about any of that. Right now I have to have something to eat, and then it would probably help me to sleep a few more hours. It's almost nighttime again anyway, isn't it?"

Looking through the windows, I was shocked to see that daylight was now entirely gone and full darkness had enveloped the little village. Then I was jolted by yet another discovery when I realized that someone had turned the electric light on. I knew it hadn't been me, and I didn't think it had been Anna, either. But what could I be sure of in this strange place?

Anna might think it was fine to stay here, but I was finding it more and more difficult. My little bed in my drab, unexciting apartment in the city looked better and better to me. I replayed Anna's words in my mind and finally replied to her that we had Maria's cheese and bread as well as the few things I had bought at the store. We decided to have a quick bite and then go to sleep as soon as possible so we could wake up at first light and begin trying to leave this place. As we got into bed, I said, "Good night, Anna. And I hope I don't awaken tomorrow morning to find you tied to the wall again!"

The second room had another bed in it. I lay down on it immediately, without even bothering to take off my clothes or get under a blanket. My last thought was the odd one that the temperature in the house felt comfortable, yet nobody had made a fire in the fireplace and there was no other heat source. I was so mentally, physically, and emotionally drained that even this strange fact, along with sleeping in this mysterious house with no knowledge of where Nicolai, my suitcase, and all of my other possessions were did not stop me from closing my eyes in eager contemplation of a deep, peaceful sleep.

Suddenly, a warm wave flows over my body from above, and I can feel myself being swept through time and space by an unknown force. Although I am helpless, I feel safe, so I just surrender myself to whatever is happening. I find myself lying down again in the same room where I had been with Umai yesterday. Somehow it does not surprise me. I am in a new state of awareness in which I can fully sense my body but cannot move any part of it. There are many voices around me, but they are indistinct and I cannot understand them. I have no voice of my own.

Vibrations are running through me again and again, from the top of my head down to my feet. It is pleasurable, so I do not try to resist it. A rhythmic sound gradually enters my perception and comes closer and closer. It isn't important to me to find the origin of this sound. I am becoming accustomed to not questioning what is happening to me but just allowing myself to be inside it. I trust that it is safe for me to do this.

The rhythm pleases me and I begin to follow it. It begins to create images for me. At first they are unclear, quickly replacing one another, until finally one of them becomes strong and focused. It is a vision of an amber pyramid. It is far away at first, but it closes in on me with great speed. Its speed is frightening, and I don't know what to do.

The space in front of me turns yellow. The pyramid becomes huge, and suddenly I find myself penetrating its amber wall. There is no time to understand what is happening.

I am inside the amber, floating slowly upward within it. My body is moving in harmony through yellow corridors. It is a serene world without people, without any energies other than the experience of amber. Time is compressed here. I feel a spiral of some kind inside my body that slowly uncoils and pushes me up and up. Time spreads upward with me. The pyramid becomes a volcano and blows up. I am in the middle of the explosion, which propels me violently away.

I am safely transported into a dark forest. At some deep point within myself I am calm and accepting of what is happening. I am not afraid. I feel changed. Although some of my recent experiences have been terrifying, they have also been teachers. They have made it possible for me to detach myself and be an observer in a way I never could have done before.

"Keep going!" It is Umai's voice, and it comforts me to know she is near. There is a small path, and I follow it into the forest's depths. The colors of the forest are blue and black. From the kinds of trees around me, I know that I am somewhere in Siberia. I notice the unmistakable scent of a river and know that the water is not far away. All my senses are intense, as though the pleasures and pains of the ages have melted together in my heart. Each time my invisible feet take a step, I feel this mix of pain and pleasure. The effect of gravitation on my body has changed, and it is an effort to keep my feet on the ground.

"Keep going!" Umai's voice is stronger and more urgent, and I continue on the path. It becomes even darker. Heavy silence is now my only companion. Suddenly I seem to have turned into a very old woman, yet I feel myself to be in a very powerful state. The path leads toward a point of fire glittering in a little glade surrounded by trees.

"Why am I so old?" I ask of no one in particular. There is no answer, only Umai's voice telling me again to keep going.

My body is now dressed in long, flowing, white clothes. I walk faster and faster, drawn to the fire that burns ahead of me. Many people are gathered around it, all in the same white clothes. Some sit, some stand, and others dance around the fire. Their faces look oddly familiar, although I don't actually recognize anyone I know. Horses are tied to many of the trees around the glade. I approach the fire, and the dancers move aside, giving me a clear path to it.

Three figures are sitting around the fire, wearing flowing white dresses like my own. Their heads, covered by white hoods, are bent toward the ground. They are sitting in three of the four cardinal directions, and the path I am following leads me to the fourth direction. They do not move as I approach, but I know they are aware of me. I sit down in silence with them on the fourth side of the fire.

Gradually the rhythm of the dance around us grows stronger. Without a word or gesture among us, we stand up simultaneously. Something important is about to happen, and I allow myself to be taken by it.

I step into the fire, facing the three figures in front of me. The flame embraces my body, but I am not frightened and feel no pain. Instantly the figure directly across the fire steps into it with me. She removes her hood, and for the first time I see her face. Then her whole being transforms into a tremendous flash of lightning that lights up the entire space around us, its ends connecting the two figures still standing to my right and left.

I turn toward the figure on the left and look fully into her face. As I do, her flesh vanishes and she becomes nothing but bones—old, whitened bones. Then lightning flashes again, and I look at the figure to my right. As the lightning leaves her body, she turns into a cluster of beautiful, vibrant white flowers that seem to enclose the energy of all life. I can smell its essence in their fragrance.

Now all three figures merge together into the fire, entering the space where I am standing and integrating with me completely. Now I am bones and flowers bound together through the lightning, and my old woman's body has become that of a strong young girl.

A man's vibrant voice comes from somewhere in the circle around the fire. "We are ready to leave here. Keep the memory of what you have experienced. We will be together again." The people are beginning to leave, walking toward the horses tied and waiting for them in the trees.

"Keep going!" Umai's voice demands once again.

I am alone once more, retracing my steps down the same path that had brought me to the fire. The lightning inside me is a fine line between life and death. I understand this and feel I can use it as a gift to help myself as well as others.

When I awakened I was completely disoriented, not knowing for a moment who or where I was. I looked fearfully around and then, through the open door, saw Anna sleeping peacefully in the next room. I realized then that I had just returned to my everyday reality from another strange experience. As my final dream-feeling of balancing a point between life and death began to fade, I suddenly found myself remembering an unusual meeting that had happened more than ten years earlier.

10

I had been eighteen years old then, a first-year student at the medical school in Novosibirsk. It was a wonderful time in my life, with freedom at last from the strict rules and restrictions of high school. It was a time full of parties, new friends, theater, all sorts of new experiences. Like young students all over the world, we were discovering the first pleasures of adult life.

As medical students, we were continually going from one clinic to another, usually by bus. It was frustrating to have to waste so much time each day traveling long distances to get to our classes. One day in the middle of winter I had waited an unusually long time for my bus in a frigid wind, so I wasn't too surprised when I began to feel sick a few hours later.

By evening I had a high fever. The flu that was going around was a bad one that was sending people to bed for at least a week, so I knew I would need more than just a day or two to recover. The thought was upsetting, too, because winter vacation was about to start and I had been counting on going to a resort with my friends. If this was indeed the flu, it would certainly interrupt my plans for some well-deserved fun. Reluctantly, I went to bed to wait out my symptoms.

The next day I was lying in my bed under a warm goose-down blanket, trying to read a book and occasionally watching one of several boring television programs, when my telephone rang. It was Irena, one of my girlfriends, calling to ask how I felt.

After she listened to my complaints and said all the proper things about being sorry I was sick, we gossiped for a while about university news. Finally, just as our conversation was about to end, she hesitatingly said that she wasn't sure how I would respond to what she was about to suggest, but that she thought there might still be a chance I could go to the resort with everyone else. She said that her mother knew a healer. He worked with her at the conservatory, where he was a composer. He was said to be able to perform miracles. Her mother could certainly get me in to see him without an appointment that very night. Although I was dubious and noncommittal, my friend insisted on giving me his address and said her mother would call to make the arrangements.

I wrote down his address, not being sure what I was going to do with it. I had grown up in a family of doctors and scientists. My parents were both doctors, and my grandmother on my father's side had a Ph.D. in chemistry. Even in her late seventies, she was still running an important research laboratory in Novosibirsk. My family thought of me as a proper medical scientist, and to a certain extent so did I. From that perspective, my friend's suggestion that I see this unorthodox healer seemed completely outlandish.

But after putting down the phone, I found myself feeling increasingly curious about what this healer might do. The scientist was only one side of me. I had always felt deeply connected with my other grandmother as well. My mother's mother, Alexandra, did not have much education, but when I was a child she had seemed the wisest person in the world to me.

She lived in Kursk, a small town in central Russia. I spent the three summer months with her every year. Her little house was a place full of charms and miracles, where the word *healing* had become very familiar to me. Almost every woman who lived in my grandmother's neighborhood was said to have some sort of magical power. Some of these powers were spoken of as benevolent and healing, while others had been mysterious and scary.

One of my strongest childhood memories was of witnessing a ritual known as Calling Out the Witch. A few women from our street, suspecting another woman of performing harmful witchcraft, had carried out a ceremony to determine whether or not she was guilty. I was still a little girl, flushed with excitement, watching from a hiding place behind a wooden fence covered with thick vines.

Waiting until they thought the suspected witch would be busy and would not see them, they walked quickly along the path leading from her door to the street, hurriedly sprinkling salt along its entire length. Although the salt was completely invisible on the earthen path, the belief in the neighborhood was that a suspected maker of black magic would go to any lengths to avoid walking on it if she or he were guilty.

What I saw next was astonishing. In a little while the suspected witch left her house, but instead of walking to the street along her regular path, she followed a route so strange it seemed insane. She made a partial circle from her doorway and then made her way to the street through the high weeds with thousands of sharp thorns that grew all along the side of the road.

The neighbor women were watching from a hiding place on the other side of the street. "Aha," they said. With satisfied expressions on their faces, they went to their homes to prepare their own charms and spells to deal with her guilt.

I had lived among these women, listening to them and seeing them do their natural magic, from the very beginnings of my memory. A part of my being had been fascinated, permanently captured by the shadowy world in which they lived and practiced their mysterious arts.

So my early life had in fact been defined by two very different, almost completely opposing, ways of interpreting and responding to the various incidents of human life. I had always thought of these two different aspects of myself as being polar opposites, like Siberia and Russia, winter and summer, science and magic, and now my friend's phone call brought them back into conflict.

My inner dialogue about whether or not to take my friend's recommendation to see the healer raged on. Unorthodox healing was completely at odds with the atheistic model that was one of the building blocks of official Soviet culture. I remembered the dull, monotone voice of one of my professors: "New socialistic consciousness allows us to see old beliefs about healing rituals as what they really are—old religious nonsense."

Hearing this dull voice of "socialistic consciousness" again in my mind, I decided to see the healer. If nothing else, it would be my revenge for the irritation I had felt toward my old professor's lectures.

Outside in the cold air, I walked to the bus station and found myself at the back of a depressingly long line. I took stock of my situation. It was five P.M., the busiest time of day. Hardly anyone in Russia could afford a car, so most people used buses to commute to and from work. From the size of the line, I could hope at best for a long wait followed by squeezing myself into a small standing space on a cold, swaying bus. As I stood reflecting on my choices, a bus arrived and went right past the station without even stopping, already full from previous stops. I realized I would have to walk, fever and all, if I wanted to get to the healer on time. I set out slowly, and about fifteen minutes later I reached the appropriate block of houses.

His apartment house, a typical five-floor gray building in a new neighborhood unit, was easy to find. Seeing it reminded me that when I was younger, I had wondered if the color of people's houses might not influence their emotions, their minds, even their health. Almost every building in Novosibirsk was an ugly, gray structure shaped like a box. As I walked along, I thought about how difficult it could be to reach beyond a gray life.

The sun set early in winter, and although it was not yet late it was already dark when I arrived. I knew I had the right building, but many of the lamps lighting the stairwell were broken, making it difficult to read the apartment numbers. In my weakened state, I kept hoping the next number I squinted at would be his. The shapes of the numbers were so indistinct and difficult to read that they might as well have been moving.

Finding the correct number at last, I slowly climbed the stairs to his apartment. A very young woman, seemingly in her teens, opened the door. Seeing my look of exhaustion, she quickly invited me in. She had a small, well-proportioned figure and wore a light housedress with little flowers on it. Her long dark hair was combed and tied at the back, which left her attractive face unencumbered. "You must be Olga," she said. "He is waiting for you."

I hung my coat in the hallway and walked into the small, one-room apartment. It was a typical apartment for people of the intellectual professions—not much furniture, just a bookcase overburdened with thick, ancient books, an old table with a television set on it, an old piano near the wall, and a big unmade bed in the middle of the room. The young woman led me into the room and then went to the kitchen, leaving me alone with a man who was sitting on the edge of the bed.

He acknowledged my entrance by standing up. As his face became more visible in the light, I noticed he had short black hair, dark eyes, an intense gaze, and deep wrinkles around his mouth. What impressed me most about him when he greeted me was his voice, a deep monotone frequently interrupted by strange and apparently randomly placed stresses.

Although he was shirtless, wearing only a pair of white shorts, he seemed quite comfortable in his considerably less-than-formal attire. He invited me to sit down on the only chair in the room, and then he started to speak to me about music. He explained how the sounds of music influenced our psyches and how music could make miracles when it was created with the correct intentions.

I didn't understand half of his words, and I felt more and more uncomfortable. The combination of his strange mannerisms and his being only half dressed made me less and less confident that I had done a sensible thing in coming. I was relieved when the young woman came back from the kitchen with a cup of strong black tea. She handed it to me and sat on the bed in front of me.

"I would like to explain the symptoms of my disease," I told her, trying to construct a more familiar doctor-patient dialogue.

"Disease is only one way to work with a line of reality," she answered. "I prefer other ways. Look at me. I am forty-three years old, and my appearance reflects my way of working within my own particular line of reality."

My mouth fell open and I gaped at her, feeling dizzy. She looked no more than eighteen and could not possibly be forty-three. "You must be joking," I said, trying to focus on my thoughts in order to ignore the growing feeling of uneasiness in my stomach. I remembered seeing a picture of a teenage boy on the bookcase and noticing how much he looked like her. Now I struggled with the notion that this must somehow be her son. I could not accept this and felt even more confused and nervous than before.

"One of the things I do to slow down my personal time flow is take pictures." She got a big, well-worn photograph album from the bookcase. Then, sitting back on the bed near me, she leafed through page after page, showing me her pictures. Here she was on the beach beside the Ob River, young and smiling on a hot, sunny day. Then she was in an office, sitting at a desk, looking very serious. I wondered what her profession was. Next she was with her son and another young man in front of a country house, wearing work clothes and holding a shovel. The trees were covered with red and yellow autumn leaves, and there were mounds of them on the earth all around her.

She took me with her as she leafed through the pages of her album, traveling to different places with different people. The men she was with were replaced by other men, one happy smile after another, as the pages were turned. Her hair became longer and then shorter. She struck different poses. She smiled and she cried. I recognized her in many different places. Some I had visited myself, but the image of this woman implanted in them was somehow surreal and mysterious.

She became younger and younger in the pictures as the pages turned, and I realized she was showing me her life in reverse order, going from present to past. Now she was leaving a maternity ward with her baby and lots of flowers, looking happy and a bit confused, just beginning to see herself as a mother. Then she was a young girl at school, standing near a blackboard in a regulation black school uniform with a white collar, her brows knitted as she looked at the old teacher sitting so seriously at her desk. The last picture in the album was the first ever taken of her. She was a naked child with a toothless smile, lying on a table.

"I work with these every night before I fall asleep. I start with a picture from the present and work backward from one to another, experiencing the state of each until I get to this first picture of me as a baby. Then I fall asleep as a baby."

"Why are you telling me all this?" I was weak from the fever, and it was difficult for me to understand anything that was taking place, either around me or in the strange emotions I was feeling.

"Because you can realize it and accept it." It was the man's voice that answered.

"I came here to be cured of my flu, not to learn how to become younger." I was surprised when I heard how nervous and weak my voice sounded.

"That is only what you now believe. But of course, that is also part of it. But don't worry. You will get your recovery, as well as whatever else you came for," he said.

My earlier dizziness had returned, and the warmth of my forehead told me my fever was worsening. It would have been difficult for me to stand up. But remembering the fever calmed me a little, as I decided that perhaps my strange perceptions and feelings were at least partly just aberrations caused by the fever. Perhaps I was even sicker than I thought. I hoped it was even possible that I might soon wake up in my own bed and realize this had been only a fever dream. It was almost a pleasant thought! At the moment my vacation at the resort no longer seemed important. In my uncomfortable state, I was ready to spend almost any amount of time lying in bed if it meant escaping the situation I was in.

"Sit down here," the man said, motioning me toward the unmade bed. I sat nervously on the edge of it and closed my eyes. There was a loud buzzing sound in my ears, and my body felt simultaneously hot and cold.

Then I heard some powerful chords from the piano. I opened my eyes and saw he had taken the chair over to the piano and was playing. The music was unknown to me, but it had such a strong energy that my mind was captured and flowed into it. I felt as if I was swimming in a stormy ocean, heaved and tossed by its powerful force. I watched him as he played. He put such physical expression into his music that his whole body bounced up and down on the chair. His entire world consisted of this music.

Then it reached a crescendo of energy beyond what he could tolerate. His body was thrown violently from the piano, and he fell to the floor. I was convinced he must be totally insane. Then I realized that the final chord was still continuing, as the piano appeared to play on by itself. Now I wondered if it was me who was insane. I felt overwhelmed.

At last he stood up, took my hand, and led me to a corner of the room. To my surprise, perhaps because I was past all resistance, I felt calmer. There was a small table there, with a candle and a very sharp knife whose handle was carved with Chinese-looking symbols. He put his hand on my brow and said something in a language unknown to me. His voice grew louder, and he shouted more words I did not understand. Then he suddenly grabbed the knife and cut off some of my long hair.

"Look at this," he commanded. "Your disease is here in my hand!" He put the hair he had cut into the candle flame. I had not noticed him light the candle, and I was sure neither I nor the woman had lit it, yet somehow a healthy flame had appeared from nowhere. I experienced no shock at all at this, because at the same time I became aware that I no longer had the fever and felt completely well.

Wanting to thank him but still feeling too disoriented to think clearly, I could say only, "Thank you very much. I feel very good now. How much do I owe you?" I looked at his now impassive face, waiting for his response.

He smiled and peered closely at me. "Your payment to me will be to remember one very important thing that I am going to tell you." He took my hand and looked at it attentively. Then he said simply, "I see that one day you will learn how to control how long you will live."

I left his house confused but totally recovered. My fever had completely disappeared. I walked briskly back to my apartment, where I packed happily for the next day's trip to the student camp.

My life returned to normal after that, but the day had been a permanent victory for the side of me that was fascinated by the mysterious. My conscious mind had been able to acknowledge this experience, and so it became an integrated part of my total being.

For a long time afterward I thought about this man's last words to me and wondered what they meant. Now, here in this Altai village, I felt myself on the edge of understanding them for the first time. I knew something elusive and important had just happened to me that I could not begin to explain rationally.

I was still bewitched by my dream with Umai. The sense of real existence that had come to me within the dream reality was not entirely unknown to me. I couldn't remember when I had experienced this state in my dreams before, but the sweetly painful sensation in my heart was not new. It was associated with the feeling of "owning" my free will, knowing that even in a dream state I could control my reality through the sheer exercise of will.

A loud knock on the window startled me back from my mental wanderings and into the present moment. I jumped from the bed with my heart pounding. It was still night outside, and I couldn't see anyone in the dark street or at the window. I asked who was there, only to realize my voice was so soft I could hardly hear it myself. The knocking repeated itself.

"Who is there?" I shouted, this time too loudly.

"It's me, Olga. It's Nicolai."

I ran to the door and opened it. "Come in. Oh, God, Nicolai, where have you been? We didn't know what to think."

Anna stumbled into the hallway behind me, half asleep and looking at her watch. She stopped when she saw Nicolai. "Hello, Nicolai. How are you?" she asked.

"Better than I have been, Anna. Could someone make me some tea, please?"

"Sure," I answered. We all went into the kitchen. I turned on the bright overhead light, and Anna put a kettle of water on the gas stove. Nicolai looked exhausted and somehow different. His appearance reawakened old concerns from my psychiatric evaluation that he might indeed be mentally ill.

"Nicolai, how do you feel?" I asked, repeating Anna's question.

"Don't worry, Olga. I didn't go crazy. It is just that I am becoming a kam." He relaxed a bit and began telling us his story as he drank his tea.

"Olga, you might remember that after we parted the day before yesterday," he began, "I started on my way to come here when you went with Umai to the other house. She hadn't explained to me what I was to do. She said she would meet me later but didn't say when or where. I walked up and down the street, feeling tense and angry. At first I was irritated with Umai because she hadn't told me anything since I'd arrived. I had thought she would immediately teach me how to become a kam.

"I didn't understand why she asked you, Olga, to follow her instead of teaching me. But when you left with her, she looked at me as though I had no relevancy at all. I was actually afraid she might forget and leave me standing outside in the street. I became enraged. My body started to experience a strange sense of being hit all over. My head turned into a flame that didn't allow me to think of anything else.

"Then I moved from anger into a strange emotional state that I cannot describe but that I recognized from another time, when I was hearing the voice of Mamoush in Novosibirsk and trying to get rid of it. But now it was much more intense. I was walking up and down the street, not knowing what to do, when I heard his voice again. 'Run to the mountains!' it said.

"It sounded crazy to me, but it was as strong a command as I had ever heard. The night was pitch black, and only a few houses still had lights burning. The mountains and the forest were dark and frightening. I looked at them, and they felt full of danger.

"I heard in my mind the sounds of all the animals that roam at night. But everything was extinguished by my uncle's voice, as he shouted again above the flame in my head, 'Go to the mountains!'

"Even having spent most of my life in this country, I was still afraid to go alone into the darkness. I began to run along the street. I thought that physical movement might help me return to a normal balance. But Mamoush's voice ran with me, directing the way. I hardly noticed that instead of running toward the lights of the houses, I had turned toward the mountains.

"Soon I found myself in the dark forest, high above the village. My fear was so intense I could not stop even for a second. I thought if I stopped for even a moment, either animals or spirits would find me and kill me on the spot. I ran and ran. I went so far into the forest that when I looked back toward the village, its lights were no longer visible. Finally I exhausted my physical energy and had to stop.

"Immediately, I heard the sound of somebody's soft footsteps to my right. It terrified me. I gathered new strength and ran again as fast as I could. I thought I might die at any moment. I couldn't see any ending other than my death.

"This probably sounds strange as I tell it to you now, but at that point I was sure there would be no exit for me back to the normal world. I lost track of time. I cannot tell you how many hours I ran in the mountains, turning, jumping, screaming, losing all control of my actions. In my few brief moments of thought, it seemed strange that I had not fallen or hurt myself. Finally I became completely indifferent to my fate. Nothing frightened me anymore. Then I heard Mamoush's voice again, this time soothing me.

"'Calm yourself and lie down on the earth,' he gently commanded.

"Now the early morning light gave me a chance to see my surroundings. I was astonished to realize a whole night had passed. I noticed I was standing in a place where the winter snow had begun melting. Without thinking about anything else, I lay down in my sheepskin coat and immediately fell asleep.

"'Don't harm the grass! It is the earth's hair!' were the last words I heard.

"The sound of quiet talking woke me up. It was now full morning and the sun was shining brightly in a clear sky. Umai was there with a man I had never seen before. They were standing very close by, and they began to laugh at me. I instantly became angry at them, and my face showed it. Then they became more serious, and Umai spoke to me.

"'I knew the spirits were going to press on you yesterday,' she said. 'I didn't want to interrupt them by speaking to you. They needed to do what they did before I could come to you.'

" 'What do you mean by "press on me"?' I asked her.

" 'These are the words we use to describe when the spirits come and make a new kam run and dance around.'

" 'So this happens to everybody who becomes a kam?' I asked, feeling relieved.

" 'So you want to be special?' she replied in a mocking tone. 'There is no path for it among kams. From this day on you will be special for other people, but not for the kams to whom you will belong soon enough.'

"I still felt resistance to her, but I understood that she had come to help me, and I listened carefully.

" 'Your uncle visited me before his death. He said you would come to me one day in search of help. He asked me to teach you some things. He was sure you would come, but I thought at the time he was wrong. It is so rare for a man to move to the city and find a job there and then return to his village. Well, your uncle was right. But I am still not sure of your intentions. Are you clear about what you are about to do?'

" 'Yes. I have made a decision. I am going to become a kam.' I thought this would be enough, but she kept asking me even more questions.

" 'Do you understand that you must give up everything you have in the city? Your job, your friends, your girlfriend?' she asked, making her doubt clear.

" 'I came here, didn't I?'

" 'Yes, but you will have a completely different life from the one you would have lived in the city. Do you fully realize this? Do you accept it?'

" 'Why are you asking me all these things? Even if I said I regretted leaving the city and that I wanted to return, you know it would be impossible for me now. I can never return to the city. You are right to have doubts, because in many ways I would like to keep my city dream. It would be good to live there, to have a family and an education. But I know now that the only thing waiting for me there is the crazy house.

I don't have a real choice, do I? I am just choosing between the two evils. Which is the smaller? Yet it is more than just that. I truly desire to become a kam for the people who live here.'

"Umai listened to me intently and seemed to accept my words.

"She said, 'Well, we don't have much time. I'll give you a few things you must know in order to begin. The others you will have to find out for yourself. There are some things that, as a woman, I must not know. There are other things I may know but cannot teach you. Those things will come to you in different ways as they are needed. Your uncle, Mamoush, was a very powerful kam. He was a sky kam. Not everyone can travel to the upper heaven world. But he could do this, even in the winter when the sky is frozen. Using the mallet of his hand drum, he was able to break the ice on the sky and penetrate to the Ulgen country. I saw him journey there one time.

"'You may think that when you are a real kam you'll be different from Mamoush, just as all people differ one from the other. But that is a mistake. One of the biggest secrets is that the kam is always one. Mamoush, you, whoever comes after you, are all one kam who lives in different forms. It is a line of heritage, and the real kam is the line of heritage, not the individual kam. You may each be special persons, but in your power you are one. So now your task is to be completely open to this power of Mamoush's and become one with it. You will hear Mamoush's voice until it is completed. After that you will have your own voice and your own power. But you will have to work hard to get it. And you are right, you have no choice. The spirits have pointed you out, and it is not within your will to argue with them.

"'Come here!' She directed her command to her traveling companion, an Altai man of about fifty. I had noticed he had a slight smile on his face the whole time Umai talked to me. He seemed completely uninterested in me, but he responded to her instantly, walking over to her and giving her a big bag from which she took out a large hand drum.

"'Mamoush left this with me and told me to give it to you,' she said as she held it out for me. The oval drum was newly made and quite heavy, and its handle had been carved into the figure of a man. The wooden part was made from willow. The drumskin itself was made from the hide of an elk and was still so fresh that it had an unmistakable animal scent.

"'This elk will be your animal to journey with. We will help you now to make it alive.'

"I am not allowed to tell you much about the ceremony they helped me to perform. I don't even have a full understanding of it myself yet. But first they put me into a kind of dream. Umai's helper stood behind me, holding my shoulders and rocking my body back and forth, while Umai built a fire in front of me. The smoke was thick and stung my eyes, forcing me to close them. Soon I felt my uncle standing behind me, holding my body, and then we were hunting together. We were tracking a huge female elk that was pregnant and would soon have its baby. We had to be very silent.

"Step by step I followed the pregnant elk into the taiga. Hiding in the shelter of the forest, I watched as her baby was born. Exactly at the moment of birth, I felt my shoulders being grasped and fiercely shaken. I understood that I was to catch this elk baby and take it away. This was the purpose of the hunt. I did what I had to do as quickly as possible. I feared the mother elk, who could easily have killed me. I ran away as fast as I could, without knowing the reason for what I was doing. Then I heard Umai's voice again.

"'Place it in here!' she said. She was holding out the drum, with the man's figure facing me. I pushed the elk baby into the drum and felt how it went into it. 'Open your eyes!' Umai ordered. As I obeyed, she said in a much softer, satisfied voice, 'Your chula is caught.' She held the drum out to me, and I could see and feel the life in it without even touching it.

"I had to ask her, 'What does *chula* mean?' I had never heard the word before.

"'Chula is the live spirit force of the elk who gave her hide to your drum,' she replied. 'Now it will be your live spirit force, too. If somebody steals this drum, you will die. It is precious and must be kept close to you.' I reached out for it, and at the same time it seemed to move toward my hands. It was warm and felt as if it was faintly vibrating. I felt instantly connected to it, and I knew it was because it now held the elk's life force.

"Then I noticed something that confused me. 'The hide is that of an old elk, but I took the baby. Did I do wrong?' I asked.

"'No, you did everything perfectly. To get the chula of the old elk, you had to catch it when it was a baby. We helped you go back in time to the moment of its birth. Now the chula will serve only you. It does not have any other history. Now you know how to catch chula, and when you do it again you will not need the help of others.

"'Everything in the world has its own chula. When you are healing someone who has lost their chula, you will journey to find the chula of the sick one and catch it by the handle of your drum. Then you will bring the chula back to the present and hammer it into the left ear of the sick person. That will return their stolen chula.

"'Your chula will be your new partner and helper. It will teach you many things. Your next task is to mark your shamanic territory by making a map of it on the elk's skin. Later I will show you how to do that.'

"By the way, Olga, I asked her why the drum in Mamoush's house was broken. She said this was because the other world where people go after death is a mirror reflection of our world. All things that are good for them here are bad for them there, and vice versa. So, if they had not broken Mamoush's drum when he died, he could not have used it in the other world.

"I spent the whole day in the mountains with Umai and her helper. They showed me many things. We had to wait for night to come again so I could make another journey. It was necessary for them to lead me through this second journey in order for me to inherit my uncle's magical territory. Umai took me through the lower world and showed me many different things there. I have learned a lot, but I'm not supposed to tell you more than this. And now I'd better relax." He sighed and then fell silent.

Nicolai's story left me speechless. I got up and went to the kitchen to wash our teacups and to reflect on what I had heard. Umai's healing ritual in the empty house the day before yesterday, my experience with her last night, her healing of Anna, her presence in my second dream, and now Nicolai's story—all of it was separate, and yet all of it was connected. What tied it all together was the image of Umai.

Thinking about all these events and when they had taken place, it came to me that Umai could not have had any time at all to sleep. She appeared to have gone from one place to another around the clock for almost two full days. How could this have been possible for her? I shook my head in disbelief, as though it might give me an answer. None came, so I just continued tidying up the kitchen.

I heard Nicolai call through the open kitchen doorway, saying, "We must hurry up. It's almost seven A.M., and there will be a bus here in another fifteen minutes that will take us to my mother's house."

"What? A bus!" Anna and I screamed in unison. "There is a bus that comes here? Why did you make us walk for hours in the snow?"

"Because it only comes once a week," he explained. "Today is the day. So it's very lucky for us. Hurry up, girls!"

When we saw it, the little bus was so old and battered it looked as if it had broken down a long time ago and was permanently rooted, an immobile metal sculpture planted in the middle of the street. But Nicolai insisted the bus was not only real but would also get us to his village if we would only hurry and get on it.

As we boarded the bus, I suddenly felt a surprising pang of grief at the thought of leaving Umai. "Nicolai!" I blurted out. "What about

Umai? Will we see her again? Did she leave a message for us?" Before he could reply, the bus began its journey out of the little village into the even more ancient woods.

"I don't know where she is. She said nothing about it to you?" When I didn't answer, he asked, "Are you waiting to receive something from her, Olga?"

"No," I replied, feeling disappointed. Umai's impact on my life was finally reaching the surface of my mind.

"I have something to give her," said Anna. "I want to pay her for my healing. Would you give her this money for me, Nicolai?"

"No, I cannot. She will not accept it. If she needed it, she would have told you."

As the bus lurched slowly along, we settled into our seats, making ourselves as comfortable as possible. There was almost no road for the bus to follow, so instead of walking in the snow for hours, we spent nearly the same amount of time sitting in the cold bus as it jolted awkwardly through the mountains. In the hush that fell over us for most of the journey, I asked myself over and over what my meeting with Umai had signified for me.

I was doing my best to understand and integrate my experiences in Altai into the rest of my being, but it was difficult. Umai had not explained anything to me, nor had she even shown any interest in whether Anna and I were leaving or staying. This left me feeling incomplete and even created doubts in my mind about the importance of what had happened. I wondered if what had seemed so startling and meaningful for me had been just an everyday event for Umai. But if so, why did it still seem so important to me?

11

We arrived at Maria's village to the familiar sound of excited barking. Maria's big chestnut-colored dog was happy enough to see Anna and me but jumped even more energetically around Nicolai's legs. Perhaps he sensed that Anna and I were only visitors and would soon be leaving but that Nicolai would be staying on to keep him company.

Maria invited us into her home with the same warm hospitality she had shown before. She was more relaxed than on our first visit, but there was an unmistakable air of sadness about her. Her attention was concentrated on Nicolai. She looked at him as only a mother could, searching for signs of the changes she feared had taken place. For the first time, I realized how Maria might feel about her son giving up his life in the city to become a kam, and it made me sad to see the normally cheerful Maria looking so worried. In an attempt to distract her, I decided to ask her about Belovodia.

"Maria, have you ever heard anything about a place called Shambhala, or perhaps Belovodia?"

She kept silent for a few minutes, as though trying to remember. Finally she replied, "I have not heard much. Someone told me, though, that Belukha has always been considered a special place like Belovodia."

My heart beat a little faster at the thought that she might be able to tell me more about this place that so greatly intrigued me. "What is Belukha?" I asked.

"Belukha is the tallest mountain in Altai. The top is always covered with snow, and it is very difficult to climb. Many have died trying to conquer it."

She stared thoughtfully at me for a moment. Then she said, "If you like, I will tell you the only story I know."

I responded quickly, "Oh, yes, Maria. I would love to hear your story."

"There is a legend among my people that once upon a time the goddess Umai and her husband, Altaiding Aezi, the ruler of Altai, lived in the far North. One day a giant fish monster named Ker-Dupa turned the earth upside down. The climate in Altai had always been warm, but after Ker-Dupa changed the earth's rotation, it became very cold here. Altaiding Aezi traveled to the sky to ask the High Burchans, the most powerful spiritual beings of the time, if they would help. While he was going from one Burchan to another in an attempt to find Ulgen, the highest of them all and the only one able to turn the earth right side up again, it was still becoming colder and colder in Altai.

"In order to save her children from freezing, Umai turned their souls into stones and cliffs. She did this with her only two sons and with four of her six daughters. Then she took the other two daughters by their hands and went with them, searching for warmth, to the southernmost part of Altai. She and her daughters froze there, becoming a mountain with three tops. The middle top is Umai's head, and the two smaller peaks on either side are the heads of her daughters. This mountain is called Belukha."

"That is an interesting story," said Anna, sipping from her cup of herbal tea. "I've heard that Belukha has also been called Ak-Sumer, or White Summer. It is a name taken from Buddhist mythology, and it represents the mountain that is the center of the world."

I sat quietly listening, excited to learn that the name *Umai* apparently had been the name of one of the high goddesses of ancient Altai.

Having finished her story, Maria began to prepare our supper. She added wood to the fire in the stove and gathered the cooking ingredients from the cupboards of her small kitchen. After she had finished cooking, she took small pieces of the lamb and potato dish she had made and placed them deliberately into the fire. At the same time, she said some indistinguishable words under her breath. I recognized this as an Altai ceremony honoring and feeding the spirit of the home fire before each meal. After the fire had embraced the pieces of food as a symbol of our gratitude, we were allowed to eat. We ate silently, for the most part, each of us reflecting on our own thoughts.

After dinner, Nicolai walked with Anna and me to Mamoush's house again, where we were to spend our last night in Altai. Tomorrow we would begin our return trip to Novosibirsk. The room didn't seem quite so ominous to either of us this time. Everything appeared to be as we had left it, so perhaps it was our perception of it that had changed. I made my bed on the bearskin, once again giving the real bed to Anna. I actually preferred the firm bear's hide to the softer bed in which Mamoush had died, but I decided not to mention this to Anna.

As I lay down, the broken drum again commanded my attention. Turning myself toward it, I lay watching it for some time. Gradually I began to sense a vibration in the darkness around me and the drum. Just as I passed into sleep, I saw the small wooden man who served as the drum's handle jump out and begin to dance in the space in front of my eyes.

Soon I entered a strange state of reality in which I knew I was once again plunging into a dream, but I also knew that this time I would be able to control the state of my awareness.

I am moving in a tiny dark room. There is a sensual joy in my moving body. I feel the freedom of my will, but at the same time I sense that someone else's will is present and has influence over me in this space. Somehow I know it is a man. I look around. Whoever is with me knows I am looking for him. He does not want to be discovered, so he remains just out of my vision. I am not yet afraid, but I am irritated that he might have more control over my actions than I do. I can sense that he is watching me, and now I am beginning to wonder if I am frightened. Perhaps I might not be in control of my dream after all. Finally I stop myself from thinking about it and concentrate on moving around the room, getting used to its darkness.

"It's me, Olga. Nicolai." It is the hoarse voice of an old man, but I recognize it as Nicolai's. I turn toward the sound and see him sitting on a chair in the middle of the room. It feels strange to see another person in this state of conscious dreaming and to be able to speak to him as if we were both fully awake. I get to my feet and begin walking around him.

"Why are we here?" I ask. My own voice also sounds different. It feels as if we are communicating with each other in pure thoughts, and yet there is still the feeling of pronunciation and speaking. Waiting for his answer, I continue to move. Somehow I know that if I stop, this reality we occupy will dissolve.

"I am here to remind you of one thing."

"I hear you, Nicolai. What is it?"

"She is a rare, powerful woman. She did everything she was meant to do simply and quickly. She did what everybody else here does, but she is more honest and brave than most."

These words are spoken in the same hoarse voice, and Nicolai is still sitting in the chair in front of me, but somehow the words come into my perception from high above. An intense feeling of nausea and aversion settles into my stomach, and I am vaguely aware that there is cause for fear in the words. I realize I have heard these exact words before. There is no actual memory of them yet, but my body's panicky response makes me grasp for times, dates, and circumstances. Before I can reach them, an unbelievable change takes place in my perception. Suddenly I realize not only that I am inside my own dream, but that within that dream a second vision is pushing its way into my mind. These two conflicting realities are interacting with each other, fighting each other to dominate my awareness.

For a moment, the new vision seems pleasurable. The graceful figure of a beautiful woman dances in the space in front of me. But suddenly she turns toward me, and I see her face. I know this face. Instantly I remember her look of hatred and the triumphant stare from deep within her hypnotic blue eyes the first time I saw her.

"She is a rare, powerful woman," says the voice, and now I recognize it as the same hoarse voice from my nightmare in Novosibirsk. Helplessly, I succumb once again to the feelings of fear, weakness, and anger that had overcome me at the unexplained death of this woman who had been my patient.

Her death, with my nightmarish vision of her hatred, had been one of the most frightening experiences of my life. But those feelings had been nothing to the horror that now attacked me in this new dream. My earlier dream with her had been pushed aside, but in it there had been a kind of protective boundary between me and the dream reality. In the new dream, this boundary of safety has completely vanished. My entire being is paralyzed by the horrible image of this woman. I know she possesses unlimited power, and that she can terrorize me at will.

Again and again I open my mouth to scream, but the words echo only in my head. No sound comes forth. All the control I thought I had of my will, my voice, and my actions has been stripped away.

"You can be taught the same power that she has."

"No! No! I don't want it!" I scream silently from an inner space, shaking my head back and forth, trying to reject everything in the

dream. In the next moment I am back within my body in the cold-
ness of Mamoush's house, lying on the hard bearskin. An extremely
painful sensation between my eyebrows stabs me violently awake.

The dream had been so frighteningly powerful that I dared not risk closing my eyes again in the unfriendly darkness. I lay nervously awake the rest of the night, becoming cramped and stiff because I had to lie on my right side to keep from seeing the small wooden figure in the drum.

When the first morning light finally filtered in through the tiny window, relief flooded my entire being. I was mentally, physically, and emotionally exhausted and wanted nothing more than to return to my safe and predictable apartment in the city. I needed my old familiar surroundings again. I needed normalcy in my life. I wanted only to be traveling home.

Anna awakened about an hour later. Soon we heard Nicolai's knock on our door, and we went gratefully with him to Maria's house. The bus was scheduled to leave at two, so we had plenty of time to eat breakfast and visit.

After breakfast, Nicolai took me aside and said, "Olga, I have something important to tell you."

My first thought was that he had decided he really did need psychiatric help after all. "Go ahead, Nicolai. I will listen to you," I replied.

"May we walk a little bit?" he asked.

As we went out into the morning street, I was surprised to find that being alone with him reawakened all the unpleasant sensations from the previous night's dream.

"This may sound strange to you, Olga, but I want to ask you to stay here with me for a few more days."

When he saw the startled look on my face he cut himself off, realizing how I had interpreted his request.

"Oh, no, that's not what I meant," he blurted out. "I am not inviting you to stay as my girlfriend. No. My intention is quite different. Actually, it is not even my own wish that you stay. Until a few hours ago, I fully expected you and Anna to leave today. I expected it, and it was fine with me. But early this morning I heard Mamoush's voice again. He said you must stay."

Despite Nicolai's protestation, I was still unsure of his intentions. I had no desire to remain here, and his little speech annoyed me.

"You know, Nicolai, I am touched by this invisible, unprovable communication I seem to have with your uncle. And I don't want to insult you in any way, but I really prefer it when people are honest and take responsibility for themselves. If you want to ask something of me, please do it on your own. I do not believe in the ability of the dead to be so involved in the business of those who are still alive."

"That is because you don't believe in death."

"What do you mean, Nicolai?"

"I mean that your feet have been set on a path that can lead you to tremendous power, but you are walking away from it, either because you don't want to make the effort or because you are afraid."

Along with a change in his style of speech, I noticed that his voice had also become deeper, and he looked as if he was almost in a trance. It aroused my professional curiosity, so to get him to continue, I replied, "Well, just what kind of effort do you think I should make?"

For the first time since I had met him, Nicolai showed real anger. His eyes glittered coldly, and his words to me were sharp.

"First, you must stop playing your stupid games with me and accept my words directly. You are using self-deception to avoid believing that what I'm telling you is very important. You will see this if you will just stop hiding from it."

This tirade sounded so unlike the usually mild Nicolai that I couldn't answer him. I just stared at him with a stunned expression on my face.

He continued, "You have been given a chance to receive knowledge and power offered only to a chosen few. This knowledge would enable you to relieve any problem you might face in your life. Nothing could ever bother you after you accept this knowledge."

Finally I recovered enough to speak again. I interrupted him, saying, "Well, Nicolai, it really sounds attractive. But would you please tell me why I am the one who has been chosen for this important knowledge?" I was certain he heard the sarcasm in my voice, but his face remained serious and thoughtful.

"Olga, there is no place for empty talking right now. You have a choice. This choice will not be given to you twice, so please think carefully before you throw it away. To answer your question more seriously than you asked it, you have been given this opportunity partly because in your profession you have already made great progress in learning how to help others by relieving their problems and diseases. But have you found even one truly reliable tool you can count upon unfailingly to decrease human suffering, much less to cure it? No matter how hard you try, many of your patients continue to be sick, unhappy, and frightened. Have you succeeded in your search to stop suffering? Be honest now and answer me."

"Well, I suppose I have failed, as you are trying to point out. But what would you suggest?"

"Nothing, except for one very simple thing. I want to explain to you that the source of all pain in this world lies in our inability to accept death. The greatest human suffering known lies between our knowledge that we all must die, and our desire to live forever."

"Nicolai, I could give you my own little lecture on this theme. But I still don't see your point."

"My point is not in giving you lectures, but in my ability to teach you how to accept death. You are not ready for this yet. Because of that, you are not ready to help others in this way. But if you will stay with me a few more days, I can give you an important gift that you will need if you truly wish to relieve the suffering you see all around you."

For the first time since Nicolai had begun explaining his offer, a feeling of excitement came over me. Little by little, he had erased my skepticism. I no longer doubted that what had happened to me had been important and had influenced me deeply. To abandon it by going back to the city without the final experience Nicolai was offering seemed much crazier than staying.

Nonetheless, my rational mind still realized that my staying here would look very strange to Anna and Maria. I didn't know how to explain it to them. I felt very confused.

"All right, Nicolai. I must say you have made a good argument. Perhaps it does make sense for me to stay a little longer, as you suggest. But I need time to think about it. Can you wait an hour while I make my decision?"

"The hour is not a problem, Olga. But I know you have already made your decision." With these words, he walked briskly toward Maria's house and disappeared into it.

I began to walk slowly in the opposite direction. Everything around me seemed extraordinarily calm and peaceful. The motions of my walking, in correlation with the natural beauty of the mountains, began to put me into a dreamlike state. I wasn't thinking about anything in particular, nor was I conscious of any specific feeling. I had a strange sense that the world was dissolving around me. I kept walking toward the mountains that began just outside the western boundary of the village. Where the street stopped, a narrow path continued up the hill.

The sun was in front of me, lighting my way. I walked higher, my exertion making me warmer as the path became steeper and narrower. I took off my coat and carried it over my arms. Finally I reached the level where the snow still totally covered the earth. The tall green trees stood between the white of the snow and the blue of the sky. The trees began to close in on the small, dark path and I stopped, suddenly realizing I was in a wild place and that it was time to think about where I was going.

"Olga." The silence was broken by a deep whisper from my right. Fear rose up in me, and I nearly screamed. Had someone followed me? Turning quickly toward the sound, I saw Umai standing near a small crevasse in the snow. She stood in the bright rays of the sun, and its reflection off the white snow was so blinding it was difficult for me to see her clearly. But it was definitely Umai, and a sudden happiness flooded up in me, as if I had met a loved one again after a very long parting. I ran to her across the snow.

"I am so glad to see you again, Umai!"

"I came especially to see you," she answered in fluent Russian.

"I am very honored."

"Olga, we don't have much time. I came to tell you some things of importance that you must understand. I am aware of everything that is going on with you right now. I know Nicolai has made a suggestion that you are considering. It is because of this that I came here to see you.

"Listen to me carefully. You are in the middle of an immense struggle. Your conscious mind couldn't absorb even a thousandth part of what is at stake, so I am not counting on your understanding. I ask only for your belief."

I felt complete confidence in her, and the look I gave told her I would believe whatever she was about to say.

"Be attentive and listen," she continued. "This struggle began so long ago that you wouldn't believe me if I told you a date. Time is not as simple as you think it is. For now, you need to hear only that time has spirals, and that when two spirals come together, humanity will go through a great change. This is happening now."

Reaching toward me, she touched my hand softly and gestured for me to follow her. She moved toward the crevasse. So did I. We moved over bright snow that gradually turned into ice. The glittering of the sun's rays from it was so strong I could hardly see.

"Listen to me carefully. I want to show you something." She stopped at a place almost inside the crevasse, where there was nothing except snow and ice. "I want you to lie down right here."

"Where?" I couldn't imagine that she meant the cold, inhospitable spot where we stood.

"Right here on the ice."

I looked at her in disbelief.

"Put down your fur coat and lie down on it. You'll be fine."

I followed her instructions, but at the same time my scientific mind was trying to reassert itself. I wanted to understand more about what was happening before I agreed to it. What would my psychiatric colleagues have thought of me if they could have seen what I was doing? It confused me to think about it. But as I lay down, the serenity of the sun and the crystal blue sky erased all my doubts. I breathed in the fresh air and felt the warmth of Umai's hand as she placed it on my forehead.

"Close your eyes now, and follow my story. We are not bound to the earth. Your breathing is a gateway to places far beyond this land, and even beyond this body you inhabit for the moment. Don't allow yourself to be caught up in your fear of losing yourself. Let your breathing be its own life, and let it be free. Trust me. Follow my story, and I will follow you. You are protected."

Perhaps it is the bright sunlight doing something to my vision, but the inner space in front of my closed eyes is getting darker. Then it turns into an emptiness that I begin moving through with incredible speed. There are some flashes of light from my right and left and then all around me. I no longer hear Umai's voice.

I realize I am moving among the stars. Soon one shaped like a polygon approaches me. I hold one of its points in my hands. The star is turning around its axis, and space and time turn along with it. I sense that I am about to arrive at a new dimension of my being. When I feel I am directly above the place I am supposed to be, my hands let go of the star. Immediately I fall into another reality, so rapidly that the transition is instantaneous. Before I know what is happening, I am already standing comfortably within this new reality, fully aware of my surroundings.

I am in a small room with a few men. They are taking something out of a box resembling a safe. It is an old, dried mummy of a man, held together with threadbare bandages yellowed by time. They carefully place him on the floor in the middle of the room. As I watch their graceful movements, I begin to sense a flow of energy within me. In the next moment, I understand that it will lead me toward what I am to do with this dried body.

I experience everything in kaleidoscopic flashes, like a motion picture changing from one scene to another so quickly that there is no discernible transition between them. Now I am kneeling near the mummy, unwinding his bandages carefully to keep the original forms of his dried muscles from separating from each other.

To my right is a cup containing salt. I take some with my left hand and make a white cross with it on the mummy's face, from his forehead down to his chin and then across his two closed eyes. As I do this, I can feel the sensation of it as tangibly as if it is my own face I am touching.

To my left is a cup with earth in it. Using my right hand, I take this earth and make a black circle around the white cross.

I know the mummy must be brought to life and that I hold the knowledge of how to do it. I must begin by giving him the wish to live. I breathe deeply over his body, creating this wish for him with each of my breaths. I sense his response by the appearance of desire in his male nature. It creates a tempest of energy that will launch him into his new life.

Although he is now eager to reexperience the enjoyment of his physical body, he is not yet fully prepared for it. His mummy's body must first be transformed in such a way as to become a bridge into his new existence. One of the other men hands me a torch. Its flame writhes with such great heat and intensity that it frightens me.

Then I remember something important about the torch, and my fear of it vanishes; I remember that my body is not under the control of fire. Calmly, I put my hand directly into the flame. The two merge painlessly into one, because the nature of my body and the the nature of the fire are one. I run the torch over the mummy until no place remains untouched by flame. Then a voice from above me says, "Now he is ready to be born."

Instantly the room begins to fill with fog. I know that my time here is coming to an end and that the fog has come to separate me from this reality. Just before everything dissolves, I hear my voice saying, "Wait! Wait! Show me how I came to my own birth."

The room is half filled with the fog. The fog lessens for a few minutes, and through it I can see my own immobile form stretched out on the ground. Three figures are bending over me, guiding my present life force as it gradually flows into my body.

The image ends abruptly, and a man's voice speaks to me. "We could not let you see more than this. It would have made your heart suffer. You did everything correctly today. Go back."

I don't remember where I am, and fear fills me again. I don't remember anything at all about myself. I hear myself screaming. Then a soft, warm hand touches my forehead. Slowly, I begin to remember things. I am with the woman who takes care of me. I breathe softly in relief.

Umai begins to talk. "Here is something you must know. The kams were supposed to keep only one line of immortality, but instead there are more. You and Mamoush belong to different lines. Olga, you must leave here today. If you stay as Mamoush is requesting, he will try to destroy your line. He keeps his own line going by using other people's deaths. This is what kams have always done. His immortality exists because of the other people who die. You are an important catch for him. He plans to teach you how to accept death, and as a consequence he intends for you to refuse immortality. But that is not what you are meant to do. You are to accept immortality."

My body becomes incredibly heavy as I listen to her. I cannot open my eyes. I cannot move even the smallest muscle, yet I am still able to talk to her.

"Wait. You said Mamoush. But Mamoush is already dead. He didn't make any suggestions to me. It was Nicolai."

"There is no difference now between Mamoush and Nicolai. They are the same. Time is not as simple as you think it is. You are not only Olga who works as a psychiatrist in a Siberian clinic. There is something else about you, something you have to figure out."

I feel a chill go through my body. Perhaps I have caught a fever. I remember that I have been lying on ice for I don't know how long. The earth begins swaying under me.

In the distance I hear the sound of a galloping horse. It grows louder and louder. I can feel the pounding of its hooves upon the earth. Then a white horse comes into view. Its entire being emanates a passionate energy.

A voice says to me, *"Get up on his back and ride away!"* and I notice for the first time the small but powerfully built young woman standing beside the horse's head, holding his bridle. My attention moves from the horse to the woman's bare arm, which is entirely covered with tattoos. I have never seen anything like them. Tattoos of unknown animals circle around and around one another from her shoulder to her wrist. As I stare at her, the animals gradually begin to seem more familiar to me, although I don't actually recognize them or remember where I have seen them.

For a moment I am afraid again. "Umai! What does this mean? Why are you doing this to me?"

I hear her voice once more. "Because I have ancestors from both lineages. I have to help you make a choice. Nobody except me can do this for you."

"So it is possible to belong to two directions? If you can do this, then it must be possible?"

"I am indeed of two directions."

The horse and the dream dissolved, and I was awake. I knew a distant noise had awakened me, but I did not know what it was. I wondered how long I had been lying on the ice. Then the noise came again, and I recognized Anna's worried voice. She was wandering in the lower foothills, calling for me. She was quite a distance down the mountain, but I could hear her clearly.

"Olga! Where are you? Answer me! We will be late for the bus and we'll never get out of here."

I got up quickly from the ice, threw my coat around my shoulders, and looked for Umai. There was no trace of her. I felt an urgency to leave and started to run. The hill seemed longer than I remembered, and my breath came in difficult short bursts by the time I reached Anna's side.

"Are you crazy, Olga? Where have you been all this time? God, you look awful, completely out of your mind. I will have to take you back as a patient instead of a friend. The bus is already loaded and ready to leave. The driver said he would wait only another few minutes. Come, let's run."

"Wait. I have to get my baggage," I said to her.

"Your luggage is in the bus and may be leaving this very minute without us. Come on, Olga. We must hurry."

From the look on the driver's face, we had reached the bus just in time. There were only a few passengers, but they looked angrily at us as we started to climb aboard. I felt bad that we had kept them waiting in the cold so long.

At the last minute, I noticed Nicolai standing near the bus door. He looked surprised and asked, "What are you doing, Olga?"

"I'm leaving, Mamoush—sorry, I mean Nicolai."

"But I thought you had decided to stay. Are you sure you are leaving?"

"Yes."

"Did Umai come to you? Was it she?" His face was pale and his voice sounded tense. "Did you know that if she did this for you, she would die?"

"No! That can't be true!"

"So, it *was* Umai. Then she can no longer belong to the kams. She died for you."

His words had stunned me. All I could say was, "Good-bye, Nicolai. Please give my thanks to Maria." Then the bus door closed behind me.

12

The return trip on the bus felt as if it would never end. I cried the entire journey, with Anna trying unsuccessfully to comfort me. Finally I had to ask her to leave me alone. At first she did not understand my need for distance, but eventually she fell asleep.

When we finally got off the dilapidated bus, it was only to wait hours for our train in the cold station. Anna kept glancing at me, hoping for an explanation for my behavior, but I was not able to give her one. I didn't ordinarily hide things from her, but so far I hadn't found the words to explain even to myself what had happened. It was far too soon to try to make sense of it to Anna. I would need time by myself back in Novosibirsk to sort things out.

I breathed a sigh of relief when I finally opened the door to my little apartment. I was sure that being home would help me get back into what I thought of as my normal reality. I put my bags down and went to the kitchen to make a cup of strong coffee and light a cigarette. The confusing events of the trip still seemed overwhelming to me, and I had to consciously focus on relaxing. I knew I had returned a different person than the one who had left for Altai only a few days ago. Yet here I was, looking at my same face in the mirror, hoping to regain the reassuring security of my old familiar self.

I looked through my mail, saving the newspapers for later. Eventually I snuggled into my worn sofa to read them. At first all the news seemed exactly like the same old news of the week before.

Then, as I turned the page of the newspaper, a headline reading "Science in Siberia" caught my eye. Under the headline was a large picture showing the opening of an ancient tomb in the Altai Mountains. The picture looked interesting, so I continued reading.

The article described the discovery the summer before of the tomb of a young woman. She had been about twenty-five years old when she died. She had been buried high in the mountains, in a rocky crevice that during the brief summer had been filled with icy water, which had then frozen solid again each winter. The archaeologists believed the woman had probably been a priestess in a forgotten religion that had existed between two and three thousand years ago. Her tomb had acted as a deep freeze for millennia, keeping its contents in a remarkable state of preservation. A gift of meat had been placed at her side for sustenance on her voyage to the spirit world, and when it was thawed, it still had the texture and unmistakable scent of mutton.

The picture and description of the tomb reminded me of the scene where my last encounter with Umai had taken place, and as I read further my heart began to beat faster.

According to the article, one particular discovery in the tomb had created a great archaeological sensation. The woman's arms had been covered with tattoos of strange symbolic animals circling her limbs and merging into one another. Her tattoos had turned out to be in the same style as those found on another mummy, that of a man whose tomb had also been found in Altai nearly fifty years earlier. Like the woman, he was also considered to have been a priest from an ancient religion.

Instinctively, I was certain this was the same woman who had come to me in my dream. Dizziness took over my body. I put my legs up on my small sofa and lay down, knocking newspapers and mail haphazardly to the floor. I put a pillow under my head and closed my eyes.

In a voice that sounded calm only because of my fierce determination to make it so, I said to myself, "I do not wish to think anymore. I need to sleep. Please just let me sleep the way I used to, with no more strange dreams." Saying this did nothing to calm me, but I continued, insisting on keeping at least my voice composed. "Just relax and don't think of anything."

"That is right. This is not the time to think. You have other things to do." The words are spoken in a strong male voice, yet they sound as if they come from inside me.

"Oh, God! What is happening?" I shriek, terribly frightened.

"You are simply dreaming. Calm down," the voice commands. Surprisingly, I do feel calmer. Perhaps the voice is right. I have simply fallen asleep without realizing it, and this is only a dream.

"There are things you must learn now. What would you like to be told first?"

"I want to hear the most important thing I can understand in my present state."

"Good. Follow me." I accept his voice as that of my teacher, so when I see the figure of a man clothed in white, I follow him without any doubts. I am curious to find out what he has in store for me. He moves decisively and soon starts climbing down a ladder that goes deep underground. This surprises me, because when I asked for a revelation, I expected it would again come through something like dissolving into the sky.

I follow as he goes deeper and deeper. As we descend it becomes hotter and hotter and grows almost completely dark. Finally I see him enter a room behind a heavy black iron door. I quickly walk into it behind him, not wanting to be left alone. Red tongues of fire circle the room. Naked men holding hammers in their hands stand near huge black anvils. I see the white form of my teacher leaving the room through another door on the opposite side. To follow him I must walk through the circle of these men, and they obviously do not intend to let me pass. They grin and whisper to each other, looking at me with unconcealed contempt.

The flames almost touch my hair. The men move slowly toward me. They are silent, but I know they have decided to do something dreadful to me. The iron door closes behind me with a heavy muffled sound, closing off any possible escape. Realizing I am trapped, I begin to cry. How could I have been so gullible as to accept this devil as a teacher and then allow him to lead me here? Instead of the revelation he had promised, I know I am about to experience something really terrible.

The men are closing in on me, and I can see that they are totally drunk. Fear fills my being and has nowhere to go but out. I start screaming.

Then, from out of nowhere, a simple understanding comes into my mind. This place and the men surrounding me are all creatures of my own fears. All the images in this dream are my own. I am in control and can do anything I want with them. This knowledge makes me feel very powerful, and I step confidently toward the drunken men. The red flames fade away, and the men first shrink into small amorphous shapes and then disappear entirely. I walk through the empty room and out the other door.

The man in white is waiting there for me. "Did you remember the lesson?" he asks.

"Yes, I did." I understand now that from somewhere in the center of my being I can control what we call reality, changing it through my own will. I recall what Umai told me about the two tasks people must accomplish—to create their realities, and to create themselves. I know she has more to explain to me, and I am eager to talk to her about it.

"I want to see Umai," I tell my teacher, sensing that he knows and may be able to connect me with her.

"It is impossible for you to see her again. She did what we needed her to do. Now it is over."

"No! I want to see her!" I am screaming at my teacher. I realize how much I have missed her, and I would do almost anything to see her again.

"It is impossible," he repeats. His voice sounds exasperated, as if he is speaking to a disobedient child.

But there is no stopping me. "You are wrong! It is possible!" I insist, realizing that I am now able to manage reality. I know how to focus my whole being to bring Umai here. I do this, and suddenly she is standing in front of me.

"Well, well. You are a good student," the man says with a smile as he vanishes.

I turn to Umai with joyous anticipation. She has a wonderful, kind smile on her face, and I realize again that I would trust her with my life.

"Why have you asked me here?" queries Umai.

"I wish to know more about how we create ourselves. I am beginning to understand about creating my own reality. Now I want to learn what you meant about creating the being who lives in this reality."

"Look at yourself and the other people around you. The one and only thing everyone is doing all the time is trying to make their Self. Everyone speaks to this changing, growing being all the time, trying to shape it.

"People have three main processes for doing this. They speak inside their heads about the past, reconstructing it by changing or erasing the things that don't fit the being they are trying to create and by expanding the things that help them along. They also think of the future, imagining what they will do, how they will look, what their possessions will be, and how they will be accepted by others.

"The third thing people do is what connects them with the present. Unconsciously, they are always aware of other people's perceptions of who they are and what they are doing, and they continually react to this. Some of these reactions support their sense of Self, while *others tear it down. They see that some people are attracted to them and others are not. Most of the time, when they are around people who don't support their sense of Self, they experience what would be called a dislike for those people. Conversely, when they experience support of themselves from those around them, they create the feeling of liking those particular people. In this way, people combine the past, present, and future to create themselves. If you are attentive, you will find this happening in any person and any situation. Look around. You will notice many interesting examples of it.*

"But when you have realized all you can about this process, then you will come to the existence of the other Self, which is aware of all this and independent of it. This is your Heart Self, and it is where real freedom and magic start. It is the source of the great art of making a choice. But this is enough for you for now."

I was exhausted, and a heavy wave of dreaming soon covered my consciousness. When I finally opened my eyes again, my body felt heavy and wooden from lying without moving for a long time. I slowly massaged the feeling back into my legs and then got up to make coffee. When it was ready, I sat at my little kitchen table and slowly sipped it from an old china cup, enjoying not so much the coffee itself as its friendly, reassuring aroma. It was daylight, and through my window I could see children running after each other in the yard, screaming and laughing with delight.

The children looked distant from my third-floor window, just as reality itself felt distant and far away right then. My head was still heavy, and my body lingered in that halfway state between sleep and wakefulness. I knew I needed to think everything through in order to understand it, but I was not ready to do that now. My consciousness was still far too disordered to try to bring my life back to normal. For the time being, I would have to leave it as a job for my unconscious.

My immediate task was to prepare to go back to work the next day. There were many things to do, and I went to bed quite late. This served me well, for I quickly fell into a deep sleep that finally was without dreams.

The next morning my old routine seemed at once both familiar and strange, and I realized that I was experiencing it through the filter of my recent experiences.

Even normal vacations created conflicting feelings. At first it always seemed such a blessing to leave behind my work, with the sick faces, the unpleasant odors, the random screams, and the huge amounts of paperwork, much of it unnecessary. Then, after a while, I would be amazed to find I was beginning to miss these very same things. Eventually, I would be hoping for time to hurry along so I could get back to my hospital. Today was no different, and I felt both excited and relieved to be returning to the hospital's comfortable routine.

Walking through the familiar dim corridors, talking to the nurses and my patients, I reviewed the changes that had taken place in the few days I had been gone. The closed white door of the emergency room frightened me the moment I looked at it. Everything that reminded me of that dead woman brought anxiety surging back into me. But I was at work and had to perform my duties, so I struggled not to melt into my fear. I began to examine my patients.

Not surprisingly, I discovered that few had made any progress. The majority of them remained as living evidence of the vulnerability of the fragile human psyche.

Fortunately, Andrey, my young soldier, brought me a pleasant feeling. When I entered my office he was already sitting in the leather chair in front of my desk. He was completely recovered from his state of acute psychosis and showed all the signs of being nearly ready to go home. He sat casually with his legs crossed, and I noticed there was barely a tremor in his hands. He made an amusing contrast to the huge, rough-looking new orderly standing beside him, who was supposed to protect me from violent patients. The orderly seemed much more dangerous and violent than the friendly looking boy sitting in front of me.

"Hello. How are you today, Andrey?"

He looked confused, obviously not remembering me. "How do you do, doctor."

"Well, I guess you don't recognize me, do you? At the time we met, you were too busy with something else, weren't you?"

"Oh, God! I've been through hell. I don't know how to explain it to anybody here. Those beings from the UFO who followed me everywhere were absolutely real to me. They were terrible. They threatened me and wouldn't leave me alone. There was nobody who could help me get away from them."

"That is not exactly so, Andrey. We helped you to get rid of them with our care and our medicine. Without this help, you would probably still be consumed by your visions. Do you understand now that all those images were nothing but hallucinations?" He seemed to be contemplating my words. Then he nodded his head agreeably.

"Well, it really doesn't make a big difference what I call them. But I understand what you mean. They didn't belong to this world. I know that's right. When I think of them now, they seem like characters from a vivid bad dream. But when I was still inside the dream, it was beings in a real spaceship who were following me, making me do whatever they wanted me to do."

"Like what?"

"Like running toward the moving train and trying to kill myself. Like tearing at my clothes and trying to hurt my body. It was as if they wanted me to forget everything I knew about myself and my life. They wanted me to become their totally obedient servant."

"And you lacked the power to resist them?"

"I had no power at all. They completely filled my head. I couldn't hear any of my own thoughts anymore. I could hear only their voices."

"How do you feel about them now?"

"I guess I feel indifferent. I'm not afraid of them anymore, and they haven't spoken to me for more than a week. Other than that, I feel a little sleepy and emotionally subdued most of the time."

"That is a result of the medicine you have been taking. Now we can start to decrease the dosage and prepare you to go home."

For the first time his eyes lit up, and his round, open face looked childishly happy. He was obviously elated to hear he would be able to escape from this place soon.

I told him I would like him to begin working on the hospital grounds, helping the staff. This eliminated a major restriction in his daily life, and he would now be free to go out into the fresh air. He would clean paths and perhaps do some other menial yardwork. After a few weeks spent in isolation, the prospect of having even this small amount of freedom visibly excited him. He knew he was finally on his way back home. He left my office a happy man.

While I was going through the normal process of evaluating Andrey, I realized again how much I had changed. My perceptions had shifted so dramatically that it was as if in a few days I had gone through years of psychological studies combined with intense personal experiences. It was no longer a simple thing for me to judge someone insane or to pronounce their fantasies unreal. The indelible sensations remaining from my vivid dreams in Altai had shaken my understanding of reality. Having been acutely aware of my own conscious participation in these visions, it was no longer such a simple thing to mark the boundary between dream and reality. What was true and what was false? I didn't know anymore.

Many years of inexplicable experiences had been compressed into a small fraction of time, and they had given me a wholly new understanding of human potential. Or more accurately, they had given me a whole new set of questions and doubts about my old perceptions. Something was transforming within me. I could feel it, but it wasn't yet ready to take shape fully in my mind. This would take time, if indeed it would ever happen at all.

In the meantime, I no longer felt confident about my understanding of Andrey's disease. Even as I tried to reassure him that his frightening visions had been only the hallucinations of his diseased consciousness, doubts arose in my mind. I now entertained the possibility—even the probability—that reality might actually manifest itself in more complicated ways than we know. My old rules and beliefs could not have covered even the thousandth part of what I had experienced in Altai. I sensed that I was swimming in a tremendous, unexplored new ocean.

Looking out the window, I was reassured to see the old rusting trolley car still lying in the middle of the grounds. The peeling blue paint that covered its corpse made a pleasing counterpoint to the bright blue of the spring sky. I reflected that perhaps this inscrutable old wreck might be the one secure constant in my reality.

I opened my journal and wrote down the obligatory report on Andrey's progress. I still had a lot of other work to do as well, and I chided myself for wasting time with my daydreaming.

13

A few weeks passed, and I gradually felt more comfortable with the hospital routine. My work, which had always been very satisfying to me, now seemed almost brand new.

One morning a cheerful, alive face suddenly presented itself in my doorway. "Hello!" it said. "Are you the doctor I'm supposed to see?" Not waiting for an answer or an invitation, the rather short, middle-aged man wearing a dark blue business suit entered and stood in front of my desk.

"My name is Mr. Dmitriev. I'm a physicist from the academic city. Here is my order for hospitalization."

As soon as he mentioned the academic city, I realized that he was one of the intellectual elites. "Academgorodok," as this scientific city was called, had been built as an experiment by the Soviet government in the early sixties. They constructed comfortable cottages in a beautiful Siberian setting and invited the brightest minds from all over the Soviet Union to settle there. The purpose was to develop a new Soviet science. The people who went there worked under the best conditions in the country. The most advanced scientific equipment and technology were available to them. Even people not directly involved in the research, who worked only in menial positions, could purchase the finest food with ease and had comfortable beds to sleep in at night.

The center fulfilled its promise, becoming the source of some of the greatest theories and technological advances of the time. The people who lived there were highly intelligent and lived in an atmosphere of democracy and freedom of mind that enabled them to express their individuality. This gave them an unmistakable presence, a mixture of confidence and openness.

I could feel this presence in the man who stood before my desk. Now he pulled out his hospitalization order, a piece of paper he had wadded up and jammed into his pocket, and presented it to me by tossing it casually onto my desk. Then, not waiting for any word from me, he took a seat. I had a feeling that he was playing a game with me in which he was delicately balancing himself on the boundary between harmless joker and impudent lout.

I looked at the piece of paper he had thrown so carelessly in front of me. It was from his local doctor stating that Mr. Dmitriev had a neurotic syndrome of somatic genesis and that we were ordered to care for him in the hospital.

"Are you going to treat me using hypnosis, doc?" he asked mockingly. His eyes were laughing, but the rest of his face had a kindly look that showed he meant no harm with his humor.

I realized I was communicating with someone who had the ability to shift back and forth among different faces of his personality, but I did not experience the familiar and painful sensation of discovering a schizophrenic.

"I hate to disappoint you, Mr. Dmitriev, but I won't treat you with hypnosis. In fact, I will not treat you at all. Your hospitalization order is to the neurosis ward. This is the regular psychiatric ward. You must take your order back outside and then go to the second building on your left. The doctor who will treat you will be there."

"No! I can't believe this. It is unfair! I can tell immediately that you are the doctor who could help me. Why aren't we living during the czar's time, when I could have hired any doctor I wanted, without any territorial or other damn regulations?" he shouted dramatically. Then, lowering his voice, he added, "But maybe it's better this way. The salary I receive as a prominent physicist would not be enough to hire a doctor. I can barely afford to support even myself. Good afternoon, doctor. See you later."

When he left his face was totally serious again, without even a shadow of his joking irony of a few moments before. "What strange people psychiatrists meet," I thought, and then forgot about him until my night duty the following week.

One doctor was always required to remain available throughout the night, to be responsible for the existing patients as well as those admitted after regular hours. The duty was rotated among the staff, and my turn came about every two weeks. Some nights turned out to be so busy that there was no chance for sleep, but the arrangement had the advantage of providing the opportunity to work with patients other than my own. Some of them were interesting, and I liked the experience. It also helped financially, because we were paid almost twice as much for night hours as for our regular day hours.

That night my rounds through the hospital's wards started out uneventfully, requiring only a few simple changes in medication for patients whose condition had changed. Finally, I reached the entrance to the neurosis ward. Mr. Dmitriev was standing beside the open doorway, looking as unsurprised to see me as though he had known I would be walking down the hallway any moment.

"How are you, doctor?" he asked. He was calmer and much more polite than the last time I had seen him.

"I'm fine, thank you. And it seems you are feeling much better?"

"I'm much better. Do you have a minute to talk to me?" he asked.

"Well, if you really need something from me, of course I will," I replied.

It was a strict rule that doctors had to meet with every patient who asked to talk to them during night duty, and I wondered what special challenge Mr. Dmitriev's bright mind might have concocted for me.

"Then let's assume, doctor, that I need your help."

I asked the duty nurse to open the regular ward doctor's office for me. She stopped what she was doing and walked down the corridor to a black wooden door with a sign reading "Dr. Fedorov" on it. She found the key among the assortment she carried and opened the door.

I walked into the office first. Other doctors' offices always looked more formidable and less comfortable to me than my own. In this case, it could also have been that Dr. Fedorov's reputation was influencing me. He was known for routinely doing mysterious, risky procedures with neurotic patients whom others had given up as hopeless. No one disputed his results, which were incredible, but because of his secrecy no one really understood how he did it.

"Come in, Mr. Dmitriev, and have a seat."

As before, my invitation came too late. Mr. Dmitriev had already entered the room, seated himself comfortably, and was waiting patiently for me to sit down before he spoke. I ended my musings and looked at him expectantly.

"I'm afraid the reason I asked to talk to you may seem strange at first. But I ask you to try to hear my words with understanding.

"I do research in the field of quantum physics. My laboratory is involved in studying the phenomena of reality. I would even say that I, by the means of my profession, have been put into a more direct relationship with reality than anybody else. I have a great deal of freedom in what I do. Most of my exploration of reality involves experiments in physical science, but we have also begun using techniques based on human perception and the subconscious mind. I would like to tell you more about our work and perhaps have you visit our laboratory."

His unexpected invitation astonished me, but I continued listening with trained professional attention.

"There is something important I want to tell you. My long-term studies of reality have totally transformed my view of the world from what it was when I started my work. Much of my original certainty about the nature of reality gradually turned into an uncertainty that opened fascinating new doors for my work. The majority of the people in my life expect me to act within their 'normal' context of existence, and that doesn't bother me. It is one of the laws that I, as a human, have to obey. But in this present situation with you, I am allowing myself to exceed the boundary of our context as doctor and patient to tell you directly why I asked for this conversation."

He looked quite serious, and I liked this mood more than his previous masquerade. He seemed to be waiting for my reaction, so I prompted him.

"Please, go ahead."

"First of all, I don't believe that my coming into your ward was an accident at all. I hardly ever make mistakes like the one that brought me to your door. I have learned to communicate well with my intuition, and it tells me there was a purpose to your meeting me."

I wondered if I had heard him correctly. "For *me* to meet *you?*" I asked.

"Yes, exactly. I am already quite content where I am, doing what I am doing. I don't need anything at all. But I sense that you are going through some kind of very intense situation and perhaps getting close to understanding something important. There is an unusual peculiarity in your energy, and I felt it the first time we met. I think perhaps I can help you. In our laboratory, we have devised a new means of opening up channels to alternate states of awareness using systems of physical tools, such as round mirrors. You have experienced some strange states lately that you haven't found explanations for, haven't you?"

I was shocked. My voice was very soft as I answered, "Yes, I have."

"You see? And I believe you would like to continue in the direction you have begun and perhaps to reach an understanding of your experiences. Wouldn't you?"

"Yes, I would." His obvious sincerity made me trust him, and I felt safe in agreeing with him.

"Here is my business card. Call me any time it is convenient. I will be glad to show you my laboratory."

He handed me the fanciest business card I had ever seen. His name was underlined and below it was printed, "Chief of the Physics Laboratory." Although I was sure I would never actually use the card, I took it from his outstretched hand and stood up to leave. Then one last question arose in my mind.

"Mr. Dmitriev, what was the reason for your hospitalization? What kind of problem brought you here?"

"Can't you guess, doctor?" he replied, the trickster jumping back into his eyes again. We parted without another word, and I left the neurosis ward thinking that it might be a good idea for me to spend a couple of weeks here myself, to adjust my own unbalanced mind.

Later, my rounds finally completed, I returned to my own office. The ward was quiet for once as all its inhabitants slept. Instead of throwing Mr. Dmitriev's business card away, as I had intended, I placed it carefully in my desk file. Then I made myself a bed on my couch and went to sleep in the hope that there would be no emergencies before morning. As I dozed off, I reflected that it was probably the unconscious respect I had always had for physics, ever since my feeble attempts in high school to understand the theory of relativity, that had kept me from throwing Dmitriev's card away. I still had no intention of taking him up on his offer.

14

The night remained calm, and I slept in deep, dreamless peace. I normally would have woken up on my own in the morning, but my body must have needed extra rest because I almost slept through breakfast. After hurriedly eating it, I made up my couch, put my pillow and sheet into the cupboard, and got ready for my morning rounds. Then my phone rang, and I answered it with gratitude that it had been silent the entire night.

An unfamiliar voice said, "Dr. Kharitidi? My name is Svetlana Pavlovna Zaitseva. I am a district psychiatrist in one of the regional clinics."

"How may I help you, Svetlana Pavlovna?" I asked.

"I need to obtain some documents from your hospital regarding one of my patients. His name is Victor Isotov, and he was hospitalized in your clinic until about six months ago. I have been treating him here since then. You may not remember him. Could you please order his patient history from the archives and send it to me?"

"I remember Victor very well. I have often thought of him and have been glad that he hasn't needed to be readmitted to the hospital. Is he well? Do you need his documents for his rehabilitation program?"

"Actually, Victor committed suicide last night. Now I have to write a report. As you know, he suffered from schizophrenia. He never made much progress with his disease."

I was not used to crying at work. I had taught myself long ago to be emotionally detached from the fates of my patients. But Victor had been special. My first response was to blame this woman for his death, but I knew I had no right to do that. Perhaps she had been more competent than her words made me guess she had been in her treatment of him. In any case, I couldn't talk to her any further and needed to get off the phone as quickly as possible. I found myself saying, "Excuse me, I'm very busy right now. Please give me your phone number and I'll call you back in about an hour."

"Don't worry," she replied. "There is no need for you to spend your own time on it. I'll call your head nurse and ask her to take care of it. Thank you." She hung up, and I knew she had sensed my anguish.

Victor Isotov had been only twenty years old when he was sent to our hospital from a special kind of clinic. These clinics had existed all over the Soviet Union for many decades. They were devoted to the treatment of criminal patients, especially those who were considered dangerous. We did not know very much about these clinics because they were run by the Ministry of Internal Affairs instead of the Ministry of Health.

Among the major crimes in the Soviet Union, one of the worst was defined by Article 70 of Soviet legislation. It dealt with anti-Soviet agitation and propaganda. Most criminals convicted under this article became the functional equivalent of dead. The only difference was that they were not executed but instead had to go through the horrors of "special treatment." Many were lost to the world forever, and most of those who returned were permanent psychological invalids.

Victor Isotov had been one of those rare exceptions who had been given the chance to return to society. After two years in the mental horrors of Kazakhstan's special clinic, he had been sent home to Novosibirsk and sent to our hospital for treatment. He came to my ward carrying with him the label of "sluggish schizophrenia," a catch-all diagnosis that could be applied to almost anyone who didn't fit the government's social criteria of normality.

Those given this diagnosis, even though they might well be completely sane, suffered the same terrible consequences as those with any other diagnosis of schizophrenia. They were stripped of nearly everything valuable in their lives. They lost their jobs and their friends. They were not allowed to go to school or to participate in any social organizations.

The main syndrome in Victor's history, according to the notes his last doctor had made, was "metaphysical intoxication." His chart read, "The patient expresses abnormal interest toward the particular literature of a philosophical, religious, and metaphysical character. He states he could spend the whole day reading books without having any other interests. He doesn't have many friends because his criteria for friendship are very high. His speech is fanciful and intricate. He expresses anti-Soviet ideas. He believes that Soviet society is imperfect and could be improved in many ways."

Victor's crime—his insanity—was that at the age of seventeen he had decided life in the Soviet Union could be made better and that people should have more freedom. He had made simple, handwritten flyers trying to explain how these changes could be accomplished. He had placed the flyers on the walls in a few public places in his small town.

The chain of events that followed was typical. The local department of the KGB arrested him, a psychiatrist's consultation was arranged, the resulting diagnosis of schizophrenia was taken to the court, and the court consigned Victor to special treatment.

I wondered why he had been allowed to go home at all. Perhaps they had finally realized how ridiculous it had been in the first place to label him a dangerous threat to society, or perhaps they had decided he was cured. When he came to me, he certainly hadn't looked dangerous at all. He had a thin, white neck, and his eyes always looked meekly down at the ground. His voice was soft, and he showed all the signs of deep depression.

Victor had been my first patient from a special clinic. I discovered that he was afraid of everything. He was completely cooperative and obediently answered all my questions. The problem was that all his answers had been carefully memorized and rehearsed. They were always given in short, formal sentences that were repeated without change. "I was sick. I understand it now. I want to continue taking my medicines to prevent the disease."

There was only one time that I saw even a trace of remembered animation in his face. He had noticed a forbidden *samizdat* book that had been secretly reproduced for me on a copying machine by a friend. It was by Sri Aurobindo, an Indian philosopher and mystic, and I normally kept it hidden in my desk. After Victor glimpsed it, our relationship slowly began to change. It was the beginning of his trust for me. It was the doorway to a very long, complicated process to help him recover as many fragments as possible of the person that had existed before his so-called special treatment. I relied a lot on antidepressive and detoxicating drugs, constructing at the same time a subtle bridge for him to return back to society and himself.

Victor no longer thought that society needed changes, probably because he had simply given up the idea that changes could ever happen. I never heard him say anything that could be imagined as an anti-Soviet idea. He had been biologically trained to avoid such themes. But gradually he began to see a foggy vision of a future for himself.

It sank in that he had been extremely lucky to be released from the special clinic and to have at least a chance of making a living at some simple job in his town and of returning to his beloved books. He realized that his earlier hopes to pursue an education were buried forever, and I never tried to persuade him it wasn't true. The universities would be permanently closed to him. This realization had been traumatic for him, with his bright mind and eagerness to learn. Even after the two years of destructive treatment he had been through, he still had a passionate hunger for knowledge. This became the tool I tried to use to bind him back to reality. I pointed out to him how many classical books he hadn't yet read, how many exciting scientific discoveries he could still learn about, even through his local library.

I feared what might happen to him once he was discharged, so I kept him hospitalized as my patient for as long as I could. But the hospitalization couldn't last forever. One day his mother, a single woman who worked as an accountant for a local factory, came to take him home. Although she was middle-aged, she was dressed provocatively, in the style of a much younger woman. Her attempt to recapture her youth was as obvious as it was unsuccessful. My previous attempts to involve her in her son's rehabilitation had all failed. She had made it clear that she had little time for anything but her own private life and that she had trouble reconciling her image of herself as a temptress with being the caretaker of her sick son. Even the word *schizophrenia* brought an expression of disgust to her carefully made-up face.

After his release, Victor had written me one short letter telling about his attempts to find a job. He had been rejected at the few places he had tried, but he still hoped to find something. He also mentioned that his mother had sold all his books while he had been gone.

I hadn't heard from him after that, but I had thought of him often. A few times I had been on the verge of contacting his district doctor, but then something more pressing had always seemed to intervene and I would put it aside. After that I had been preoccupied by my trip to Altai and its aftermath, and I had forgotten about him until today.

Now Victor had taken his own life, and I felt as if he had taken a piece of my own with it. Indeed, after the first shock had passed, I discovered that the news left me feeling not only sadness but also a sense of loss more profound than could be accounted for even by the strong attachment I had felt for Victor. I tried again and again to analyze my peculiar state of mind and to figure out what it was that I was losing.

Finally I understood. After coming back from Altai, I had tried to continue my professional life exactly as before, setting aside everything that had happened in Altai as if it had no bearing at all on anything else. The pathetic tragedy of Victor's wasted life had made me realize I could no longer pretend my life was divided into two separate parts.

It was clear to me that without consciously admitting it, I had become a different person. My trip to Altai had transformed many of my most important beliefs and perceptions, and it made no sense at all for me to continue my life and my work as if nothing had changed. I could no longer justify just living a so-called normal life as a successful psychiatrist in the state clinic. There was absolutely no choice about this if, as I had always prided myself in doing, I wished to live my life with my inner honesty intact.

Victor's death was the catalyst that made me see this, and I promised myself to remember it whenever I might be tempted to compromise—to fall back into my old narrow-minded life. This would be my last tribute to my former patient. My decision gave me a huge sense of relief.

15

A few days later I took Mr. Dmitriev's card out of my desk. I knew he had already been discharged from the hospital, so I dialed the six digits of his work phone. He answered it himself and recognized my voice immediately. I told him I would like to accept his invitation, and we made an appointment to meet at his laboratory two days later. Visiting the institute required special permission, so he would be waiting at the main entrance to let me in.

When I arrived he was standing near the main door of the white, nine-floor building in which he worked. He looked completely different than when I had last seen him in the neurotic ward. He wore a long black coat, carried a leather briefcase in his hand, and seemed much taller than before. As we walked through the lobby it was clear from the way his colleagues treated him that he commanded their respect. Once again, I was astonished by his chameleonlike ability to transform his persona so easily.

We took an elevator to the seventh floor and walked to his laboratory through a series of long, empty corridors with rows of identical doors lining its sides. He stopped when we finally reached the very last door on the left. The modest sign above it said simply, "Laboratory." As he firmly pushed the door open, for some reason I suddenly realized that I still didn't know his first name.

"Hi, everybody," he said in a joyful voice. His tone told me that the three men coming toward us were not only his colleagues, but good friends as well. "This is Olga," he said to them. "We are going to do some experiments today. We'll need your help, Sergey, to activate the mirrors."

Sergey looked at me with good-natured interest. "I am ready," he said.

The laboratory consisted of two large rooms. One was filled with sophisticated computer equipment. The other was dominated by a huge tubular apparatus made from a shiny metal similar to aluminum, with various kinds of pipes and connections attached to it. The whole looked to me like some sort of small spaceship.

"By the way," Mr. Dmitriev smiled, "you can call me Ivan Petrovich. And I hope you don't mind my calling you Olga, since I am probably twice as old as you. Have you heard, Olga, about the astrophysicist Kosirev?"

"No. I'm sorry, but I have not."

"Well, that's not so surprising. First of all, I would have to guess that physics is not included in your main sphere of interests. Is that true?"

I nodded my head in agreement.

"And second, it was prohibited to say his name until fairly recently. He was in the Gulag for many years. He was very smart and talented. Somebody in his field became jealous enough to write a letter denouncing him, so of course he was taken by the KGB."

I interrupted him. "I know how that can happen. My great-grandfather served as a doctor in the czar's army during the First World War. He wrote a report to the czar about the terrible medical conditions the soldiers had to put up with. Because of this, he was sent to Siberia and punished there for many years. His son, my grandfather, was also a medical doctor in a big plant in Siberia. He wrote a report to Stalin's government about the inhumane conditions suffered by the plant workers. He was found guilty under the political articles and was also sent to the Gulag. He was let out only after Stalin's death, almost twenty years later, and lived only one year after that. I never knew him."

"It's the same story as Kosirev's, it seems. So you know that the brightest minds were often kept in the Gulag along with the priests, shamans, and hardened criminals. Kosirev spent many years there. He had some special contacts with Siberian shamans in the Gulag, but he never talked much about it.

"Eventually, after his return from the concentration camp, his main scientific interest became the theory of time. He devised brilliant experiments that enabled him to develop a complex theory of time, proving that time has a substantial nature. It has its own solidity, which changes according to the configuration of the globe. Consequently, time is more solid or less solid at different points on the earth. Of course, it is completely impossible for us to detect this with our normal human abilities of perception, but his sophisticated apparatus was actually able to measure the differences. This proved his mathematical theories about how the substance of time could actually be changed.

"You have undoubtedly noticed this large and, I am afraid, rather peculiar-looking apparatus in the center of the room. It is a tube made from a special combination of polished metals that act like a mirror. We have learned that this is one of the ways in which we can alter an individual's perception of time. In ways we do not yet fully understand, the mirrors work to transform time and space for the person inside them. Does this make any sense to you?"

"Yes. I think so." I actually understood little of what he had said, but I trusted him and was ready to explore his theory. "I will need your instructions about what to do."

"Yes, of course. Don't worry," Dmitriev replied. "We will tell you everything, step by step, as we go along.

"First of all, take off your boots and then sit inside the tube in any position that makes you comfortable. Sergey will give you some headphones, through which you will hear recorded sounds that should help relax you and open a channel to your subconscious experience.

"The cylindrical shape of the mirrors, along with the sounds you will hear, will influence your perceptions. You must try to define clearly in your mind the kind of experience you wish to evoke. Then wait for it to happen, in full awareness of all the nuances of your state of being. We won't speak to you or interfere in any way unless we feel that you need help."

I took off my boots, feeling fortunate that I had worn comfortable jeans instead of a dress. Then, as I climbed into the tube, I immediately began to feel strange sensations. I understood why they called it a mirror. I saw only rounded metal walls, polished so that their surfaces reflected vague, general images. I had never been in a space that was anything like this, and it was difficult to find a way to fit my body comfortably into it. I experimented with different positions, finally choosing an embryo pose in which I was half sitting, half lying inside the tube.

Sergey held the headphones out to me. I couldn't see his face from my perspective, and it felt as if the disembodied hand of some strange creature was reaching in to me. I put the headphones on and tried to relax as I had been instructed. A remote melody, pleasant and harmonic, flowed gently into my mind. My eyes were still open, but a particular rhythm in the melody gave me the feeling that I was already sleeping.

I tried to focus on one of my regular relaxation techniques, but the mirrored walls seemed to influence my inner dialogue by almost totally suppressing it. The feeling reminded me of my previous states of being awake and fully alert inside what I knew was a dream. In my heart I felt the same familiar sensation of intense pleasure mingled with pain.

"Olga! Listen." It is a man's voice—neither Sergey's nor Dmitriev's but a new, unknown voice. The melody merges harmonically with his voice. "I know you appreciate metaphors. Try this one. We have learned in physics that elementary particles have a dual nature that depends purely on the position of the observer. They can exist as discrete particles, or they can simultaneously be a wave. You may already know that. But you probably did not know that human beings have the same duality. We are separate particles and waves at the same time. It depends on the position of the observer inside us. Because we believe we are independent individuals, we perceive ourselves as particles that are really separated. But at the same time, we are always waves, with no boundaries at all."

The rhythm is jumping in my mind. The melody has disappeared, transformed into strange artificial sounds that I can't identify. The voice speaks to me in the rhythm of a beating heart, and I realize it is keeping exact time with the rhythm of my own heart, as if my heart were being scanned and echoed back to me.

"You should now be able to change your perception of yourself to experience that wave nature of your being. This wave is part of everything else that exists. It can travel anywhere and stop anywhere. Let your body discover the rhythm of its wave, and become one with it."

I can feel the boundaries that form my physical body becoming thinner and weaker. Then they dissolve, and my consciousness instantaneously explodes beyond its boundaries to take in all the space around me. I am now an infinite being, connected with the universe and indistinguishable from it. Linear time vanishes. All my experiences in Altai flash into my mind simultaneously.

Then I am standing in the middle of a garden of white flowers surrounded by trees. People wearing long white robes are walking silently through the garden.

A man approaches me, and I recognize him as the same man I had followed into the room with the drunken blacksmiths, where

I had gained my first understanding of how reality could be changed. I recognize him as a teacher. His calm, middle-aged face is warm and friendly, but at the same time he conveys a sense of unusual energy and decisive will. He takes me by the hand and leads me to a wooden bench placed under one of the trees. We sit down, but neither of us speaks.

The man seems to be waiting for me to speak first, but I have no idea what to say. We continue to sit silently, until finally I ask, "What am I supposed to do here?"

"You came of your own free choice, so you must need something that you hope to find here," he replies.

I remember vaguely that my intention is to seek answers to the long list of troubling questions left by my experiences in Altai. In my confusion, they all come together into one simple query: "What does all this mean?"

His answer doesn't clarify things for me at all. "It depends on the meanings you apply to your experiences. How do you want to consider them? It's up to you."

"I want to know what our meeting represents to you. Who am I to you? What is your understanding of my appearance here? What purpose does it have from your perspective?"

"Well, what do you think?" he asks calmly.

Once again I don't know how to answer. "I'm confused," is the best I can say.

"If you were free from the sources of your confusion, what would you think about your being here?"

"I would think that I'm meeting some part of my reality I haven't been aware of before and that it has great importance, not only for me but also for many others."

"That's right. Your being here is important not only for yourself but for others as well. And it's also true that you know very little about the many different aspects of the reality you live within. Hu-

mans of your time are the result of one particular path of evolution that a part of humanity had to experience. Your people developed special qualities of human nature that were mostly connected with intellectual thought. This evolutionary track required you to create a strict mythology in which reality and its laws were very rigid. These restrictions of perception enabled you to accomplish the tasks you were given, but they limited you in other ways."

"When you speak of my people as humans, does that mean that you are not human?"

"No. I am a human being, but I belong to a different branch of evolution. Your people are not the only representatives of humanity. There are streams of diversity within the human race. Each of them has a particular task. Each stream was meant to explore a different dimension of human potential. Their perceptions were separated so that each would know nothing about the others. Of course, there have been some interconnections. Sometimes whole civilizations changed their evolutionary direction and as a result discovered others and joined with them. This left mysterious gaps in the history of your people as they remember it.

"Your presence here is a sign of increasing interaction between your civilization's reality and that of others. Our time spirals are approaching each other, and the final integration of all the different streams will take place soon. The whole of humanity is finishing its cocoon stage. It is not yet aware of this, just as the caterpillar is unaware of the butterfly's body forming within it and has no knowledge of its future wings. Even the wings themselves don't understand their meaning until their first flight. The people in your reality stream have steadily been forming the solid body of a new organism, and now the time is coming for it to emerge and integrate its state of development with other branches of humanity.

"Your people will go through tremendous personal changes. It may seem like the end of the world. In many ways it will be, for much *of the old world will indeed be replaced by a new manner of existence. The psychological structure of each person will be transformed, because people's old model of reality will no longer be sufficient. Your people will experience and learn to understand another part of their being. This will happen differently for each person. For some it will be easy and almost instantaneous. Others will need to struggle through stress and pain. There will even be some people so deeply grounded in your old laws of reality that they won't notice anything at all.*

"I will tell you more. It is important that you listen to me now without interruption. I understand how much effort it may take to understand and accept what I am saying, but you must do so. You truly have no other choice except to acknowledge the truth."

As soon as he instructs me not to interrupt him, a contrary streak in my nature forces me to ask him a question. It is an important one that I feel I cannot wait to ask.

"Excuse me, but you said the different streams of people were separated, without any knowledge of each other. How is it that you are obviously so aware not only of me and my own people, but apparently of many others as well?"

"Well," he smiles, *"you couldn't wait, could you?"*

Even though I have ignored his request by interrupting him, his voice and expression are still warm.

"As individual personalities, each of us has quite different aspects of our being, which develop in their own unique directions. But remember about our Heart Self, the one that integrates every single intention of our life into the totality of meaning. The same is equally true for humanity as a whole. If you consider humanity as one entity, it still has many faces. But at the same time, it also has a genuine Heart Self that knows all the directions and integrates them. This place is here, where we sit."

A wave of excitement goes through my body. "Is this place called Belovodia?"

"It has different names as well as its own hierarchies."

Belovodia has grown and grown in my mind ever since I first heard of it, and now all the mystery and excitement of my experiences in Altai come pouring back at his mention of it. I wait for him to continue, eager to learn more that would help me clarify my persistent mental confusion. I focus intently on every word, trying to memorize each detail as he continues.

"From time to time in the past, civilizations from different reality streams crossed over and met with yours. Each time this happened, it became a stimulus for further evolution. If you looked back and examined the history of your world from this perspective, you would see these points of interconnectedness quite clearly.

"Now it is nearly time for the biggest change of all. You will soon intersect and experience many of the different facets of human nature that have been developed within other human reality structures. These people will know as little about your beliefs and ways of life as you know of theirs. Because of this, these differences will be uncovered gradually. In the past your people have usually protected themselves from such contacts by giving them mystical names and treating them as myths. But mysticism is quite different from and far more real than your assumptions about it.

"One of the most important lessons to remember is that the entities you will meet from other reality streams—worlds—are human beings like you who simply have experienced a different form of evolutionary growth. This means that their perspectives and experience can be understood by you and that each of you will also be able to integrate into your civilization the advantages developed in the civilization of the other. It will be a time for conscious interactions.

"In your own particular case, there are always a few people within each evolutionary reality stream who are able to penetrate dimensions other than their own. You are one of those who has been able to cross these boundaries. You will experience more such crossings. In the same way, there have been others who lived in evolutions parallel to yours and who learned to embody themselves in the space of your reality.

"And as I have said, when your people intersect with those from another world, it will not only change your people's beliefs, it will transform the very structure of their being. At first your people believed almost universally that they lived in a reality that existed wholly independently of their perceptions. To believe so gave them knowledge and many important tools. But gradually, as your time spiral began to converge with those of other worlds on different evolutionary tracks, first your so-called mystics and then even your scientists started to become aware of mechanisms through which reality and even the future events of one's own life could be influenced. You created many new theories and tools in trying to explore this phenomenon and to reconcile it with the rest of your beliefs.

"The next step will be one you are already taking, which is to realize that there is another self that creates one's personal reality. Your Heart Self, your genuine self, is the one responsible for this creation. Each person must experience it to understand."

Although at one level I realize that what he is telling me is extremely difficult to absorb using rational understanding, somehow it seems clear to me and I take it all in without much effort. I wonder momentarily if his presence is creating a channel of understanding beyond verbal explanation.

"Your 'ego' is not as bad as many of you have learned to think. Actually," he smiles, "there can be better or worse egos. People are different. But the phenomenon of ego was itself the main foundation for getting your evolutionary tasks done. Your civilization could not have taken the form it did without ego. The reason why so many now feel it has harmful effects and should be diminished is because they unconsciously foresee the next step of evolution. Your society will be able to recognize and integrate with others only by finding and entering its Heart Self. Ego is not a helper anymore."

"How can I speed up this process?" is my next question.

"By working at it and practicing it. Many esoteric schools in your world have created different ways of preparing people to do this. Their practitioners went through these transformations. In the past, instruction of this kind was a privilege obtained by only a few chosen people. One of the important changes in the time ahead is that transformations will be experienced by many people all around the world at once. There are already signs that point to these changes, and your culture must be prepared for them.

"You, Olga, are particularly connected with one of the changes. The event took place in Altai, but it is geographically related to Belovodia. You are already part of this story, without having much memory of it yet. But this will come in its time."

My heart starts to beat faster. I have a feeling that he is close to telling me about something very important to me personally. At the same time, I notice that the sun has become so brilliant it is very difficult for me to look at him without squinting my eyes until they are nearly closed. The ridiculous idea comes to me that I should have brought my sunglasses.

If he is aware of my irreverent thought, he doesn't show it. He continues, "Some of the ancient tombs opened by your scientists have actually been tombs belonging to other dimensions, other evolutionary streams. These are not just material, physical manifestations. The seemingly dead inhabitants actually have alive intentions. They serve as channels of communication with other human dimensions. These channels were created with the specific purpose of making contact with your people. There are only a few places on earth where this has been done. Altai is one of them. Your journey there was not a chain of accidents. Every step you took was intended to awaken a memory. And you are moving along your path.

"The tomb uncovered in Altai was intended to be opened only when the coming transformation was ready to be widely visible. The fact that it has already been opened means that the changes will be speeded up naturally. It means that more and more people will experience the need for a new existence. Many different teachers and schools will emerge, but they will all point in the same direction.

"To speed up your individual progress, you must follow the correct path. Some of the guideposts for this path have been integrated into the morals and structured religions of your society, but when this was done they were always combined with simple social needs to control people's behavior. Now you need to extract them in pure form. You must learn these rules so you can teach them to others who also seek transformation."

The glossy green leaves of the tree behind our bench are slowly swaying in the field of my peripheral vision. Birds are singing so harmoniously that I can't help but notice how heightened my senses are.

"Now I will tell you the First Rule. It is extremely important, and you must remember it. The First Rule is that every choice you make in your life, from the most important ones to the smallest everyday decisions, must be tested by conscious questioning. For each decision you face, you must ask yourself if the choice you make will satisfy five necessary attributes. If even one of them is absent, you must look for another direction. In this way, you will always find the right path. These five attributes are truth, beauty, health, happiness, and light.

"When you make a decision in this manner, you can always be certain it is the right one. You will be in touch with your genuine self, your Heart Self, and you will create for yourself an invincible power of will. This is the first lesson. Live by it, and very quickly your *life will be changed. Then, when you are ready, you will be told the Second Rule. For now you should go back."*

First I must ask him another question, one that is very important to me.

"What can you tell me about Umai? She spoke to me about the choice between death and immortality. I want to see her again to ask more about that."

"Umai's past is from the shaman's line of reality, but she is also a part of Belovodia itself. Shamans have always been messengers between human dimensions. They are people of action. Not all of them understood exactly what they were doing, but Umai always did. She helped you mostly by working through your emotional nature. That is why you feel such a strong attraction to her. She told you about immortality because it is connected with the Second Rule of evolution. Death is one of the characteristics of your civilization, and it will be transformed along with many other things. Umai will teach you this lesson when you are ready, after you have learned to practice the First Rule.

"Don't worry about her. The one who told you she had died was trying to deceive you. She cannot die. She is a part of Belovodia, and death is not.

"If you really wish, you can see her now. But because of your attachment to her, she might be manifested to you very differently than before, in order to teach you. This might be harmful to your feelings for her. Are you ready to part with your affection for Umai?"

I don't feel ready to lose my deep and intense attraction to her, so I answer, "No. I guess I am not prepared for that."

"It is good that you can see where you are so clearly. Now it is time for you to leave."

He puts his hand on my forehead, and a strong, warm energy touches me. Bright flashes of light startle me, and I open my eyes for *a few seconds. I am in a different place, but I can't remember exactly where I am. A different man's hands take hold of my wrists and gently help me out of the tube.*

As I became more awake, I saw Dmitriev and two of his co-workers standing around me looking serious and tired. Dmitriev reached out and took a notebook from me, which I noticed was filled with my handwriting.

"May I look at this, Olga?"

"What is it?"

"It is your notes. We gave you a pen and paper after you had begun your journey. You were writing all the time, though you may not remember it at all."

I left him the notebook and walked slowly to the bathroom down the corridor. When I looked in the mirror my face frightened me. A dark red triangle covered it from the middle of my forehead down to my nose. When I instinctively touched it with my fingertips, it felt warm. It was the birth mark I had been born with, which the doctors had told my mother was a form of vascular tumor. Fortunately, it had disappeared when I was just a year old except for a brief, faint blush of pink that would occasionally be visible when I was under a great deal of stress or emotional trauma. It was so slight that nobody else had ever noticed it. Now I saw that it was intensely dark, as my mother had described it when I was born.

Still feeling confused, I turned on the faucet and washed my face with ice cold water. I had always hated the smell of chlorine, but now the slight trace of it in the water helped me complete the transition back into my body. I concentrated on the thought that I was standing in a small bathroom at the Institute of Nuclear Physics. Soon I would take a bus home to my apartment and what I hoped would be a night of restful, dreamless sleep.

By the time I walked back to the laboratory, the triangle on my face had almost disappeared. Nobody mentioned it, and in fact they hardly seemed to notice my return. They were all standing together around a desk that had a map of Altai spread out on it. They had marked a point in the southern part of Altai, and I recognized it as the location of the tomb from which the mummy of the priestess had just been uncovered. They were talking to one another about it.

"Look, it is close to Belukha. Do they have anything published yet on that mummy they found there?"

"Not really. I don't think anything has been published except a few small newspaper articles. I believe a team from *National Geographic* magazine has visited the site and interviewed the people who excavated it. Perhaps they will publish something on it soon."

Then they all turned and looked at me in unison. Dmitriev handed me back my notebook. "This was fascinating, Olga. I have been waiting for something like this to happen. Your experience today has helped me tie things together in new ways. From my work in the physics of reality, I had already felt that time and matter were on the edge of something important; a time of changes. But my knowledge of this came from mathematics and from studying energy fluctuations—vibrations, if you will. But I've never approached it at all from the perspective of human psychology and awareness. You have opened a new window for me.

"Your notes about the tomb in Altai were also very interesting. You know, there was a lot of mystery around its opening. Some of the local people were very much against it, predicting big disturbances if it was opened. It was the same many years ago, when the opening of another tomb revealed the mummy of a man from the same period, with the same kind of tattoos. The fact that both the man and woman were Mongolian priests of some unknown religion made their presence here quite baffling, since all the other remains that have been found in the Altai area were of Indo-Europeans belonging to the Pazyryk culture.

"So, as your notes recorded, their uncovering may be the beginning of something very important. Let's see what happens next. But you look very tired, Olga. You need to go home and get some rest. Do you want me to drive you home?"

As much as I appreciated his offer, I declined. I was indeed tired, but more than that, I wanted to be alone so I could think. The day's events still seemed overwhelming to me. The only certainty in my mind was that I had done the right thing in coming here. I sensed that it might not be the last time, because there was no longer any question of turning back; of denying the new direction that had so suddenly taken over my life and expanded it in ways that might take years, if not decades, for me to even begin to absorb.

16

The long bus ride back to Novosibirsk passed quickly as I continued to reflect on my strange vision in Dmitriev's mirrors. I didn't fully understand everything that had happened, but one important realization was that while shamans held one key to the door of knowledge leading to Belovodia, the knowledge itself was universal and could be reached in different ways. This excited me, and I knew I had taken another step closer to my dream.

It was very late when the bus finally reached the city, and I walked quickly to my apartment through the dark and deserted streets. Despite the hour, I was still filled with a strange excitement. Sleep was impossible, so I fixed myself a quick snack of bread, cheese, and tea. Then I sat down at my desk, turned on my small table lamp with its emerald green shade, and took out the notes I had written in the lab.

I read again the few pieces of wrinkled paper covered with hastily scrawled words. The pages fascinated me as they lay on my desk. The handwriting was my own, but I had no memory at all of having written it. The pages were a material manifestation of the greater mystery that was overwhelming me. Thoughts of Altai and Umai crowded into my mind. Everything I had experienced, beginning with Anna's first phone call about Nicolai, came back to me as clearly as if it had happened yesterday. I picked up my pen and started to write.

My words flowed almost without thought for hours, as if I was in a trance. I stopped only when I realized the sky was beginning to get light. I had been completely oblivious to the fact that my blinds were still open, the window beside my desk covered only by a transparent lace curtain. I closed the blinds and finally went to sleep.

The next day, the day after, and for many days that followed, writing down my experiences in Altai became the most important and pleasurable part of my busy schedule. It also opened up an entirely new perspective on my journey. At first I was consumed only by the need to create a record of the outward details of the strange events I had experienced, but gradually I began to realize that the frustration, confusion, and tension I had felt during and after the trip were directly connected to my insistence on seeing everything superficially.

My first direct experience with Umai, when she had led me to the discovery of the space of the Spirit Lake, had been the true starting point for my journey. I realized I hadn't yet fully learned the sacred and demanding art of keeping the balance between outer and inner tasks. The more I forced myself to interpret my experiences in terms of their underlying meaning to my inner self, the more evident the hidden levels of my journey became. Everything Umai had done had been another lesson to help me explore a different dimension of this inner space.

Umai had taught me well and continuously, just as she had promised. Page after page in my new journal illuminated this for me. The many threads of her first teaching logically integrated all of the experiences that followed, as soon as I separated them from my outer gaze and looked inward. I became able to see the powerful wisdom and profound knowledge behind the sometimes frightening, sometimes pleasing images and symbols of my journeys.

I understood the concept of the Spirit Lake and saw that for most people this space had been invaded and consumed by their preoccupation with the material world. I understood the importance of accepting that we have both the ability and the responsibility to create not only our own reality, but also the self that lives within that reality. I understood the process of inner dialogue through which we form personality. I saw that the First Rule was a powerful tool for creating a metaposition in any situation, a position independent of one's environmental influences, reflecting only the pure essence of the internal observer.

Each of these concepts became fascinating additions to my psychiatric training. I saw how easily the concepts incorporated and even developed some of the most modern theories dealing with the structure of the human psyche. The most intriguing idea of all to me was the existence of another self, which I referred to in my journal as the ontological or core self, which could be connected to the great art of making a choice. I felt that this concept held within it a huge potential for a new understanding of the intriguing questions surrounding human nature, evolution, and purpose.

As my writing moved step by step through each of my experiences, I finally came to my work with Dmitriev. I felt that it held the final key to everything else, even though I didn't have a full understanding of it yet. I still wondered if this mysterious country, Belovodia, was a real place or if it existed only in some hidden dimension of our minds. Neither could I resolve intellectually the apparent connection among the archaeological tomb discoveries in Altai, time spirals, and the diversity of human evolutionary streams. And what did it mean that the "seemingly dead inhabitants of these tombs actually have alive intentions"?

These questions remained unanswerable without additional knowledge, so they became the temporary ending of my journal. With a feeling of gratitude toward Umai, I placed my notebook onto the bookshelf. But I still felt an energy connecting me to it, telling me clearly that it was still far from ended, and perhaps only beginning

A few nights later, I had a strange dream.

I see myself entering a small room. A table made of dark, polished wood sits in the middle of the room, and several bookcases stand in a semicircle near the walls. I look around, trying to understand where I am.

A tall, slender woman comes into the room and smiles at me without saying a word. She has black skin with a strange underlying yellow tint, unlike any human skin I have seen before. Her face has an oblong shape with attractive, regular features. Her thick, straight black hair has been formed into an intricate, high hairdo that emphasizes the grace of her body. She moves toward me with a mysterious smile.

I know that her language is totally alien to me, but we have the ability to speak to each other through the energy of our thoughts, without using words.

My mind forms questions. "What am I here for? And who are you?"

Her reply immediately sounds in my mind. "You are here to go through an important operation. I am a facilitator for it."

The word operation *makes me feel uncomfortable. Flashes of a remote childhood memory arise on my inner screen. I remember a huge white room with a big window in its ceiling; the muted voices of the nurses from behind surgical masks that transformed them from my friends into frightening alien beings; the nauseating smell of ether that permeated my clothes and remained with me for days as an unpleasant reminder. Finally, I remember the figure of my mother operating on the patient's face or, more accurately, doing some kind of precise instrumental magic on the place that was supposed to be the face but that to my perception was a pale, deformed spot covered in scarlet blood that pulsed out from somewhere inside.*

When I was about nine years old, my mother had taken me with her to the hospital where she practiced medicine. She had performed facial surgery of some kind that day, and the nurses, who all were my friends, had allowed me to put on a surgical gown and secretly enter the operating room. Hidden behind the nurses' backs, I had watched the entire operation.

"Don't fear." The woman's thought enters my mind. "This operation is different."

As in any dream, the connections among different parts of my experience have their own peculiar dream logic. So I'm not surprised to see myself next, without any transition, lying on a table surrounded by men and women. They all bear the same black skin and geometrically regular facial features of the first woman I had encountered, who now is standing behind me. She says something to the people around me in her own language. Then I feel her long, thin black fingers touching my forehead, and I relax.

My entire body feels as if it consists of some plastic substance that can easily change shape. The woman's fingers dance quickly in the space before my eyes, occasionally touching my skin. An energy is being created inside me. My body begins to turn, as if I am rolling up into some kind of a ball. The movement goes faster and faster, and I become a rotating spiral spinning into a final focal point. Then it is finished. The billions of cells forming my body have rearranged themselves, joining together into a single large, round cell containing all the information that exists about me.

I am vaguely aware that the people are doing something with me. I don't resist, because I understand they are healing something deep within my structure. It lasts for a while, and then I feel myself lying on a solid surface. It is completely dark around me. I am aware that I am still dreaming and that dream logic still applies, so I'm not surprised to hear someone laugh softly just to my right.

"Who is here?" Somehow the sound of my voice influences the luminosity of the place I am in, and it becomes lighter as I ask my question.

A woman is sitting cross-legged on the floor near a corner of the room, holding a pipe. It is Umai, and her pipe is the same one I had seen her smoke in Altai. Although she is smoking it, I don't smell any scent of tobacco. For some reason, this surprises me more than Umai's presence.

Instead of greeting me, she asks a question. "Do you remember why you came to Altai to see me?"

"I'm afraid not."

"Then try to remember," she says softly but insistently.

At first I remember only my initial reason for the journey. "I guess Anna asked me to accompany her," I reply. Then I remember more. "And, yes! I also wanted to learn some healing methods from you."

Umai continues to laugh softly as we talk, and she is slightly swinging her body rhythmically from side to side. Somehow I have the distinct impression that she can dissolve into the air at any moment she chooses.

"Can you stay here with me for a while and not go away?" I don't want her to leave, and I am fishing for some guarantee of her presence.

"Can you?" Umai asks in reply. She squeezes her narrow Mongolian eyes almost shut and exhales a cloud of smoke toward me from her pipe.

"I guess I can."

"So can I."

I smile in relief, while at the same time trying to keep an appropriately solemn expression on my face for the moment of teaching I anticipate.

Umai giggles loudly, as if she sees something very funny. Then she seems to remember something and becomes serious again, talking a little faster as if she is now in a hurry.

"All right. You say you came to Altai to learn about healing. This is absolutely correct. Healing is your destination.

"You think that everything started for you from your experience in the space of your Spirit Lake. This is not exactly so. The teaching of this space was actually the second thing. Your true beginning was when I allowed you to make those fish on the wood swim. This enabled you to experience the healing power for the first time. But I have to admit you have done well in integrating these two lessons with those that followed.

"Now I want to answer a question you haven't asked yet, except in your mind. I do this because I think it may help you in your work as a healer. It is this:

"Diseases of the mind have only two causes, and they are totally opposite of each other. One way people can become crazy is if their soul, or a part of their soul, has been lost. This usually happens because their soul has been stolen from them, but sometimes they may even decide unconsciously to give it away, perhaps in exchange for something else they want. The second way people can become crazy is if they are overwhelmed and occupied by a foreign power.

"There are only these two reasons; nothing more. It sounds simple, but it may take you much time to learn how to distinguish the source of a disease correctly and heal it. If you are mistaken in the cause, then your attempt to heal will actually feed the disease and make it worse. You must be prepared to learn much more before you can become a good healer.

"This is why the lesson of the space of the Spirit Lake was given to you almost at the very beginning. The power to heal lies in that space. It is the house of the Healer inside all of us. At the same time, this space is also your road to Belovodia. The more you explore your inner water of life, the closer you will become to Belovodia. Am I right that you are seeking this?"

"Yes," I answer. Once again I feel a particular excitement in my body, anticipating that an important piece of knowledge is about to come to me. I feel myself a hunter, ready to catch it with all my senses.

"You are wondering if Belovodia is a real country or not. You will learn more about this later, but it doesn't really matter right now. The important thing to remember is that nobody will ever find Belovodia, either in this world or any other, except through exploring the inner self. The only road to Belovodia leads through your inner space, through expanding your self-knowledge.

"By this, I don't mean the empty theorizing with which so many people like to feed themselves. This is totally separated from the space of the Spirit Lake. I am speaking of serious, practical work. For you it will be work in healing.

"Listen to what I say next, because it is very important. Every human has a particular entity who inhabits the place of their Spirit Lake. These entities exist within this inner space, waiting at the entrance to Belovodia. I call this entity the Spirit Twin, but its name could also be Spirit Helper, Shadow Watcher, Spirit Guide, or Inner Guardian. They are really many different things.

"To begin with, they are intimately connected with the ultimate purpose given to each person at birth. They are also pure observers, set apart and invulnerable to the influences of the outer world. They watch and silently consider everything we do. They are the holders of the primal essence of our natal being. If called upon in the proper way and circumstances, they can be important helpers to us in performing actions that move us in the direction of our correct purpose. And finally, they can be our guides to Belovodia.

"There are seven different kinds of these Spirit Twins. Just seven, and no more. The seven types of Spirit Twins that exist for people are these: Healer, Magus, Teacher, Messenger, Protector, Warrior, and Executor. Understand that the last is not a person who kills, but one who makes things happen.

"One of our most important tasks is to learn the identity of our Spirit Twin and then to integrate ourselves fully with it. In this way, we come into unity with the ultimate purpose of our being. When

our lives have finally been illuminated by the pure light of our inner observer, everything we do becomes much easier. Only by discovering the nature of one's Spirit Twin, and then by coming into total association with it, can one really find and open the gate to Belovodia.

"You, Olga, are destined to be a Healer. *The operation you just went through was a first step, because unless you are healed yourself, you will never be good at helping others. This was an initiation for you.*"

"*I'm very grateful for it. I'm grateful to you, Umai, as well, for this new knowledge you have given me.* . . .*"

Umai quickly interrupts me.

"*Never mind, Olga. In some way we are colleagues now, aren't we? I'm not the worst Healer myself, as you might know.*"

She laughs and, still in her cross-legged sitting position, begins swinging her body from side to side again. This time she is doing it more strongly, and I know she is about to disappear.

Umai is already beginning to fade, but her last words to me are: "I want to give you a final gift before I leave. This gift is to tell you that you are now ready to communicate directly with the Healer who is your Spirit Twin. If you need help in healing, ask your Healer to come out and do the work for you. Don't be surprised by your actions then, even if they seem strange or even foolish. Try it tomorrow and see for yourself."

Then a small cloud of tobacco smoke was all that remained in the corner where Umai had been sitting a moment earlier. The cloud still floated in my memory as I opened my eyes in the darkness of my room and tried to awaken completely.

In my imagination, my journal almost seemed happy when I took it down from the bookshelf and began writing down everything I could remember from my dream. I was particularly intrigued by Umai's last suggestion about my Inner Healer, "Try it tomorrow and see for yourself."

I had not visited the women's ward for a few days, so the next morning I decided to begin my work day there. I shared an office there with George, the doctor who ran the ward. He was already sitting behind his desk when I arrived, and from his particularly benign smile I suspected he must have some unpleasant surprise for me.

"You look great, Olga! Fresh and full of new working energy!" he exclaimed, giving further proof to my suspicion.

"Thank you. Okay. Enough. What do you have for me?"

"Nothing in particular. There is just this one case I want to transfer to you. I think you will be glad, because you should be able to learn a little bit from it. She is a very interesting patient. I am almost making a sacrifice by giving her up to you. But my opinion is that young doctors should be given every possible chance to learn about this demanding profession of ours. And please, no objections. She is yours. Here is an 'epicrisis.'"

He handed the patient's history to me. I took it from him reluctantly, anticipating something disagreeable. I wasn't disappointed.

Patient Lubov Smechova admitted to our hospital for the first time about a month ago. Her current diagnosis is *sch., schisocarn* type of progression; depressive-paranoid syndrome.

Sch., schisocarn meant that she had a particularly rapid and malignant form of schizophrenia.

Previous medical history: From a background of long-lasting and increasing depression, the patient began to express paranoid symptoms including delusions of reference and persecution. Hospitalized because of peculiar and inappropriate social behavior. During her first week in the ward, she developed a short-term episode of acute psychomotor excitement. Motivationally unimpeded, no inhibitions or control, barked like a dog, and became completely withdrawn, with no consciousness that could be addressed. Psychomotor excitement was reduced by large intravenous doses of neuroleptics. Subsequent total amnesia of the episode.

Currently, negative symptoms predominate. The patient exhibits stable emotional-volitional flatness. She lies on her bed, indifferent to her environment, family, work, or future. Retardation in cognitive sphere. Prognosis: negative. Recommendation: immediate application for the second group of mental disability.

Most patients with schizophrenia took eight or ten years before they were assigned to the "second group of mental disability," which meant that they were totally incapable of either recovering or caring for themselves. The incredibly rapid progress of Lubov Smechova's disease was a testimony to its virulence. Assigning her to the second group also meant that there would be endless forms to be filled out, endless consultations with colleagues and committees of experts, a lengthy recommendation to be filed, and then a final hearing before a commission.

"Oh, no! It's unfair! You can't do this to me. I'm already overloaded with four criminals in my men's ward that need full evaluation, diagnoses, and recommendations to be filed in court by the end of the month. I can't take another disability case. Do you want me to have to live in the hospital?"

I almost screamed, but at the same time I knew George wouldn't change his mind. He was a very sweet old man, knowledgeable and always helpful, but also well known to the entire hospital for his unwavering commitment to have as little as possible to do with documents, courts, or complicated diagnoses. Further, as chief of this ward, George had every right to assign patients to me. So I really didn't have any choice. This woman, Lubov Smechova, was really going to be mine.

George looked at me silently, with infinite compassion, as I took her documents and left, shutting the door behind me more loudly than usual to express my irritation. I could almost see his fatherly face, still smiling kindly at me, from behind the closed door.

As usual, I found I couldn't really be angry with him longer than a few minutes. By the time I reached the office we used for patient evaluations I was calm again. The nurse on duty was Marina, and I asked her to bring Luba to me.

While I waited, I read her complete file. Her case was truly terrible. The word *schisocarn* in her diagnosis meant that her entire psyche had burned out completely, hundreds of times faster than for most other schizophrenics. I looked carefully through the preliminary psychological and psychiatric evaluations that had been done, including information from her family history indicating that some of her close relatives had suffered from the same form of disease.

Everything in her diagnosis seemed correct. She was given no hope for even a short remission, so she was supposed to be placed in the "second group," under government care, almost at her very debut into insanity. Despite my already crowded case load, there was no plausible reason for me to delay her disposition at all.

The nurse quietly knocked on my door. "Here is Luba, doctor. May she come in?" she asked.

"Yes, please bring her in," I replied. I saw how carefully the nurse guided my new patient into the room. Her movements were full of compassion as she helped Luba sit down on the chair in front of my desk. "All right, dear," she said. "Here is your new doctor. Maybe she will help you get well."

Marina's words were so clearly inappropriate that they upset me. "What is she talking about?" I asked myself. "Why is she giving this woman false hope?" My initial irritation at having Luba as a patient returned, but now it was directed toward the nurse. After thirty years in psychiatry, she should know what to say to patients in the final, incurable stages of schizophrenia. "Get well"? Hah!

I glowered at Marina as I dismissed her. "Thank you, that will be all. I'll call you to take Luba back when I'm done."

Marina left quietly, leaving me alone with a forty-year-old woman frozen like a seated statue in front of my desk. Her short, thick black hair was disheveled. Her eyes, big with a slightly Eastern, almond shape, were so empty and inexpressive they were almost unnoticeable in her face. A slight tremor in her hands was the only movement her body would allow itself. She wouldn't walk, wouldn't move, wouldn't do anything without an external push of some kind.

"Hello, Luba. I'm your new doctor."

She showed not even the slightest sign of interest.

"Well, Luba, whether you talk to me or not, I have to inform you about your present status and how we are going to help you." She was so absent it was like talking to myself.

"Whatever." Her voice had a mechanical sound totally lacking in any trace of personality or interest.

I leafed again through the pages of her history. She had been a schoolteacher, with a husband and two teenage sons. Nothing unusual. But somehow, as I looked through her records, my mind involuntarily returned again and again to the inappropriate phrase Marina had used: "Maybe she will help you get well."

This phrase played over and over in my mind until suddenly it met Umai's last words to me: "Just ask your Healer to come out and do the work. Don't be surprised at your own actions, even if they seem strange or even foolish. Try it tomorrow and see for yourself."

The two phrases coalesced in such a way that a wave of temptation rose up in me, pushing me toward an action that made no sense to the rational part of my mind. Something, perhaps the total blankness that seemed to pervade Luba's being, told me that her illness came not from occupation by any foreign entity, but from having somehow lost her inner soul. The only hope for her was to give her some kind of stimulus that would give her the will to reach outside herself, in the hope that she could find and retrieve what she had lost. I wondered if perhaps I could do this.

"There is no risk involved," I told myself. "She is lost anyway. Do as Umai said. Just give it a try. Use it as an experiment. Nothing I can do could possibly make her any worse."

Luba was sitting in front of me with the same vacant facial expression. I didn't feel any urge to say anything to her about what I was thinking, because I knew that I wasn't reflected at all in her conscious mind. I looked silently at her papers a while longer until I had made up my mind.

Feeling slightly silly, I dared to pronounce the words only silently, inside my head: "I ask the Healer inside me to come out and heal this woman."

For a brief moment there was a strange interruption in my perception. It felt as if my face, my identity, moved downward from its usual position on my head and stopped in the place of my heart. For a few seconds I actually seemed to see the world from the central part of my body, as if my heart had grown eyes and had the ability to see. This was accompanied by a strong wave of heat and excitement that went like a flash through my chest and then quickly disappeared. When it passed, my usual therapeutic machinery started working.

I stood up, walked around my desk, took the second chair, and sat very close to Luba, right in front of her.

"I want you to listen to me very carefully. It doesn't matter if you don't react to what I say, because I know there is a part of you that will listen to me and accept my words as truth. I know that you chose your disease because of some very important reason in your life, Luba. I don't have any idea what it was that you needed your disease to save yourself from, but I am sure it was a very brave decision at the time. I join you in thanking your disease for coming to you at the right time and for doing something very important for you. Okay?

"Now, Luba, I want you to listen to me even more carefully."

This sounded really pathetic to my ears, so far was Luba from showing any reaction at all to my words or even to my presence. Nevertheless, I continued.

"I want to emphasize one very important thing to you. Even though your disease once created something useful for you, your agreement with it was temporary. The problem is that you have forgotten this. You still expect your disease to accomplish something for you. But this is wrong. This is totally wrong, because the need for it has passed. It has no further value, and now it is only destructive."

I was becoming very emotional as I talked to her, as if I was part of her family, expressing the same anguish, fear, love, hatred, and shame her husband and sons were undoubtedly experiencing. I almost felt as if I was losing control of myself.

"You don't have to pay such a high price. Your disease has deceived you. It is a monster that will destroy you, your family, and your entire life. Do you know what is going to happen to you? No, you do not. I will tell you what is going to happen to you. I am certain of it. I have already seen your future, and I will tell you how you can see it, too!" I was almost screaming, and I held her hand tightly.

"Look at me, and I will tell you what you are going to be."

I shook her hand violently back and forth, trying to get her attention, but her only reaction was to give me a brief indifferent glance. Then she turned her face away and looked out the window. Still I continued.

"You are going to become exactly what Larisa Chernenko is. That's all you will be. If you are willing to agree to this, then go ahead and do it. All I can do for you now is just give you this warning."

Everyone in the women's ward knew Larisa Chernenko. She had lived there for the last twenty years. A former singer, former general's wife, former beauty, she was now a violent, ranting, raving terror to everyone, patients and hospital staff alike. Her mind was completely destroyed. She didn't take care of herself, laughed hysterically for no reason, intimidated even the most psychotic patients around her, and spent most of her time restrained to her bed because she was dangerous in her violent dementia. The straps binding her hands and feet were removed only to change her sheets or bedpan or to feed her.

Luba showed absolutely no response to my words and still sat as the same stone monument in her chair. I stood up, feeling defeated, and went to the corridor where Marina waited.

"Take her back to her room, please," I requested and then stood near the door watching how carefully Marina helped Luba get up and walk into the corridor. Marina closed the door behind her, leaving me alone in the office. I wearily put my face into my hands, trying not to acknowledge the shame and dissatisfaction I felt with my performance. But the feelings were too strong to be avoided, and soon I was berating myself for my stupid and unprofessional actions.

I wondered what I had expected when I asked my Inner Healer to come out. Certainly I hadn't expected what actually happened. The only "cure" I had tried was the trivial technique of dissociating the subject by introducing the idea that a transitory positive function for the disease had now passed. To have picked a less appropriate patient for this technique would have been an impossible task. Luba's psyche had already been totally disintegrated by her disease, and she obviously didn't have the energy or ability to accept any new meanings or symbols.

I tried to console and calm myself with the thought that perhaps my Inner Healer hadn't wanted to come out this time, or perhaps I hadn't asked it properly.

I wrote everything down in my journal that evening, discovering in the process that writing about my failures was not such a bad practice, since it helped me to accept them and gave me at least some feeling of relief.

I didn't see Luba again for the next four days because of the weekend and some emergency situations in my men's ward. On the fifth day I finally went to see my women patients. I allotted myself three hours to spend in the ward and decided to use some of it to complete all of Luba's legal forms. There was no point in delaying, and the earlier I did it, the fewer deadlines would be left facing me at the end of the month.

Marina was on duty again today. She was obviously glad to see me, and I was pleased to discover that I didn't harbor any embarrassment or negative feelings in relation to my recent fiasco with Luba.

"Hello, doctor," she said. "I was afraid we had lost you. If you hadn't come today, I was planning to call you."

"Why such a hurry? Is there something new?"

"Oh, there is definitely something new." She had an excited smile on her face as she walked with me through the corridor. She stopped outside the room with Luba and three other patients.

"What's going on?" I asked, feeling that there was something not ordinary in Marina's behavior.

"Luba wanted to see you, doctor." Marina gestured toward the room, so I turned and stepped into the doorway.

At first Luba didn't see me. She was sitting on her bed reading the local newspaper. Her beautiful, fully alive face showed interest and concentration. Her hair was carefully combed. She even wore a slight touch of lipstick. She was dressed in her own knitted dress from home, a privilege allowed only to patients cleared to go home in a few days. I couldn't believe my eyes. I stood in the doorway feeling stunned, looking at her in a mixture of awe and admiration.

Suddenly she saw me. She immediately dropped her newspaper, jumped from the bed, and ran toward me with a huge smile, as if she was greeting a long-lost friend.

"Oh, I'm so happy to see you, doctor! I've been waiting for you so eagerly. Thank you for what you have done! Many, many times thank you!" Then she stopped, uncertain that she should go on until she saw my reaction.

I was stunned nearly to the point of speechlessness. "Hello, Luba. I'm glad to see you, too. Let's go to my office, Luba. Right now, please," were the only words my shocked mind was able to find.

We walked to the same room where she had sat in front of me, as passive and inert as a stone, just a few days ago. Now she was a totally different person, alive, communicative, hardly able to restrain her energy and enthusiasm.

"You look totally different, Luba. Incredibly different. I guess you feel better now, too?" I spoke slowly, trying to adjust to my new perception of her.

"You healed me, doctor. I'm back, I'm healthy. You can't imagine how happy I am."

I listened to her, thinking over her words and trying to understand what I was seeing and hearing. Luba had definitely entered into a pronounced and totally unexpected, almost impossible, remission. At the same time, I knew there was no way the trivial piece of work I had done with her could have brought about such a result. It was completely implausible. Something different must have helped her, and I leaned toward the idea that some biochemical endogenic cycle had created her remission following its own unknown law.

"Well, Luba, I appreciate your thought that I helped you. But I really don't think my role was so important. I think your body healed itself and that I had little or nothing to do with it. I wish I could claim the responsibility, but I have to face the truth."

"You had nothing to do with it?! Please, don't say this. You were the one who pulled me out of that nightmare!" She was quite upset.

"Let me tell you what happened after you had left here last week. Marina brought me back from your office, and I lay down on the bed just as I had done on all the days before. My state of mind before then had been very strange, but at that time it hadn't made any difference to me. I was no longer 'me.' I had become something foreign, empty of all thought, emotion, or even movement. I was a dead, dried piece of hell.

"When Marina left me in your office, I could hear you talking to me. I understood your speech, but I was totally indifferent to your words. Of course, at that time I was totally indifferent to everything, even my own children. But you planted a tiny seed of interest in me when you told me I was going to become like Larisa Chernenko. At first my interest was too weak to make me get up and go look for her. But the thought kept playing in the nearly total emptiness of my head, giving me a small connection with the outside reality. I slowly turned over in my mind the question of who this person might be, and then at some point I asked Marina who she was.

"'We don't have a patient by that name in our ward,' she answered. That was the real beginning of my change. Her answer surprised me, and this feeling of surprise was the first emotion that returned to me.

"I thought about it for a while. Then I started to look at the other patients at breakfast, lunch, and dinner, trying to figure out who Larisa Chernenko might be. Finally I realized that what Marina had said was true. There was no such patient in the ward. This mystery intensified my feelings, and my interest grew as a snowball around it.

"It was so important for me to figure out what you had meant that my attention became completely obsessed with it. I couldn't think of anything else, couldn't do anything else, except walk back and forth through the corridor, among the women in the ward around me, looking over and over again for Larisa Chernenko. Finally I came to the state when my entire existence depended upon recognizing this woman. But she wasn't in the ward.

"Finally, Sunday was the day when our relatives were allowed to visit us. My own family had been so disappointed and upset by their previous attempts to talk to me that none of them came. I walked among the other patients and their relatives, still consumed by my burning desire to find Larisa Chernenko.

"Suddenly I heard an orderly's voice announcing another family member who had come to visit. 'Larisa is here to see her mother.' Hearing the name was like an electric shock to me. I went eagerly to the door and waited for her to come in.

"'Poor girl, she still comes to see her mother,' I heard an orderly say.

"'Mother is always mother, no matter what. But nothing can be done for her,' replied another voice. Then I saw the orderly walk a young girl to the room where the most violent patients were kept.

"'Tamara Chernenko, your daughter, Larisa, is here!' the orderly screamed into the room where the woman everyone called 'terrible Tamara' was kept. She had been temporarily let out of her restraints, and when she saw her daughter she began swearing at her violently, saying terribly foul things to her.

"Larisa stood in the doorway crying silently, not daring to take a step toward her violent mother. Tamara continued to scream and swear at her. Then she suddenly ran toward her daughter and smashed her in the face with her fist. Larisa ran away as several male orderlies took Tamara and tied her back into her bed. She was immediately given an injection to calm her down, but she continued to scream, spit, and swear for nearly thirty minutes until it finally took effect.

"I didn't see when Larisa left the ward. I was still standing near the wall, feeling stunned. I finally understood whom you meant and why you had used the daughter's name instead of the mother's. It was just your trick to confuse me, to give me a little piece of something outside myself to hang onto.

"Something happened to me at the very moment that I realized this. I felt as if somebody had literally grabbed hold of my hair and pulled me out of my disease. I was overwhelmed by thoughts about my husband and sons and how they must have felt about my sickness. It was as if a dam had suddenly burst, and the huge energy it released entered my body and filled it up again. I felt fully healed in just a few moments, while I stood motionless near the wall.

"And I know that without you it would never have happened, doctor. That's why I thank you."

I listened to her in astonishment. My mistake in referring to "Larisa" Chernenko had been a completely unconscious slip of the tongue.

Never would my conscious mind have been able to concoct such a strange healing strategy. But somehow it had happened, and it had worked. Luba was the proof. She was sitting in front of me, healthy and beautiful. My next step would be the very pleasant one of forgetting about her disability papers and instead completing the procedures that would allow her to go home.

I felt such incredible excitement, relief, and happiness that I could hardly keep myself from crying. Umai's advice to me had really worked! My Inner Healer had actually come out and helped this woman. I was ready to kiss Luba, to dance with her and run around the hospital telling everyone what had happened.

At the same time, the thought of telling the true story to other doctors was sobering. It was impossible even to imagine sharing the mystical concept of an Inner Healer with my colleagues in the psychiatric community. So instead of excitedly running off to spread the news, I talked to Luba awhile about going home and about her job and her future, and then I sent her to prepare for leaving.

I took Luba's file and went to George's office. As I walked along the corridor I suddenly noticed the white door to the emergency room. I realized that finally, after all the weeks following my female patient's death there and all the mysterious events associated with it, this was the first time I'd had the strength to look at it without feeling fear or guilt. Until now, I had simply avoided it, denying its existence. Now I was able to look at it again, with a feeling of victory. I knew that Luba and this woman had both been invaded by the same insatiable disease. Before, it had succeeded in capturing and devouring its prey. But this time I had beaten it.

George had just returned from lunch and was hanging his long woolen coat in the closet when I arrived.

"Ah, Olenika!" He greeted me by my nickname. "I'm glad to see you. I hear you have some very good news about Luba!"

"That is exactly right. She is going home."

"Yes, yes. I saw her. It's almost a miracle. No, not almost a miracle; it really is a full miracle. I can't find any explanation for her remission. I don't think I was wrong with her initial diagnosis. Everything was perfectly clear. And now this. Well, the only thing I can say is that sometimes, even for elders in psychiatry like me, it doesn't hurt to learn a little bit more about our profession."

Luba went home to her family. She had to give up being a schoolteacher, because the label of having been in the "crazy house" didn't leave her any choice. Nevertheless, she found a job as librarian in the local library and seemed reasonably happy with it. I followed her case for three more years, at which time she was still in a state of stable remission.

17

Despite Luba's dramatic recovery, for a while afterward my experiences in Altai still created considerable professional confusion for me. Among other things, I now found it difficult to draw a distinct line between the theoretical unreality of psychosis and the supposedly firm normality of sanity. Then, with the help of my writing and through discovering my inner healing power, my confusion was replaced by a deeper understanding of human nature that helped me become a more confident and effective doctor.

I began studying native rituals and healing ceremonies and applying them to my practice along with conventional treatment, creating new forms of therapy. The native Siberian belief in total animation—that everything in existence is alive, has its own spirit, and can be communicated with—became one of my most useful psychiatric tools. I learned what the shamans meant when they said that each disease had its own spirit.

As one example out of hundreds, the Altai people believed that wax had the property of absorbing negative energies. The healer would walk around and around the patient with a pot of hot, melted wax, chanting spells to call out the illness, while the patient stood in a trancelike state with eyes tightly closed. When the healer had withdrawn all the negative energy, the patient was instructed to watch as the hot wax was poured into cold water. The wax would form bizarre shapes as it cooled and solidified, letting the patient see and interpret in his or her own way the nature of the disease that had been removed.

To avoid controversy, I described this particular healing method to my patients and colleagues alike as an experimental new technique in projective method, and I practiced it only in the privacy of the hypnotary. The same general ruse was used with all the other esoteric practices I introduced. It was remarkable to see how everything depended on language and perspective. I could clothe almost any ancient traditional technique in modern garb, and it would automatically be accepted by those around me.

These old/new methods worked, and they strengthened the powerful new source of healing power within me. With their help, I was able to tear at least a few of my patients free from the darkness of their insanity. I now approached schizophrenia completely differently. It was no longer a vague abstract idea to me but a distinct enemy entity, an extremely clever entity with its own malevolent intentions. As I became able to recognize these intentions and to predict how they would manifest themselves, I began to be able to fight them more successfully. I now knew that even schizophrenia could be conquered, and I no longer experienced the same helpless fear when I saw it staring cruelly from my patient's eyes.

Then, as I learned more and more about alternative healing methods, my practice gradually expanded beyond working with mental patients into the healing of serious physical illnesses.

I had made a decision to try to live my life by the First Rule. I began testing each decision, both the large ones and the small, everyday ones, by the criteria of truth, beauty, health, happiness, and light. Abiding by the First Rule proved to be a fulcrum that enabled me to make decisions I could not have expected from myself before. Sometimes these decisions were very difficult, but always they proved right.

Practicing the First Rule immediately led to important changes in my political life, which before had been minimal. But the tragedy of

Victor's death made me realize I must do everything I could to protect others from repeating his fate. Despite the risk of doing so, I joined a small number of people in Novosibirsk who joined an organization called the International Association of Independent Psychiatrists. As psychiatric experts, we counseled people like Victor who had been politically repressed through the misapplication of psychiatry by the state. We succeeded in helping quite a number of these victimized people to return as functional members of society, even after they had been falsely labeled as schizophrenics.

It was still dangerous to become politically involved in ways like this that opposed the system, and many of my friends paid high prices for their activism. Before long, every member of the International Association of Independent Psychiatrists in Novosibirsk except me had been questioned and then dismissed from the hospital. But despite the risks, I never doubted my decision. I knew that in making it I had chosen truth, beauty, health, happiness, and light. I knew that it was right.

Eventually, it became my own turn to be called before the chief of hospital administration. I fully expected the same fate as my colleagues, but before entering his office I asked my Spirit Twin to be with me and to preserve the hospital work that was my life. Once again the now familiar wave of warmth passed through my chest, and there was a short flash in which I seemed to experience the world from the position of my heart. Then I opened the door and went in.

My meeting with the chief turned out to be short. For some reason, although I felt inwardly calm, I forgot all the sober answers I had prepared to defend myself. Instead, I found myself talking nonstop, compulsively babbling like an idiot about almost anything that came into my head.

After a few minutes the stern look on his face faded away. Soon he began to fidget. Before long his impatience transformed into irritation and then into an almost panicky need to get rid of me. Finally he cut me off in midsentence, telling me that I was a young and politically naive female but that he wouldn't put any pressure on my life outside the hospital and that I could go back to work. Then he waved me out the door with a look of confused relief.

My own look was also one of relief at the miracle that had just occurred. But the meeting had shaken me so badly that my entire body was trembling. I felt incapable of concentrating, so I left the hospital an hour earlier than usual and went home.

Before long, I realized that in my anxiety I had forgotten to cancel the neuroleptic medication for one of my patients. This was an alarming oversight, because this patient was at risk of developing malignant neuroleptic syndrome, a potential complication of his therapy in which his medication would interact with his metabolic system and greatly accelerate it, causing a very high fever. If it happened it would require emergency measures at best, and at worst it could even cost him his life.

I tried to call my ward right away, but all the lines were busy. Although it was against the rules, the nurses were probably using the quiet evening hours to make personal calls. Finally I gave up trying to reach my own ward and managed to get through to the main admissions office. I asked for the duty doctor, but none of the nurses on duty seemed to know where he was.

After another half hour of increasingly desperate attempts to reach my own ward, I reluctantly put on my coat and headed back to the hospital. I was in a bad mood contemplating the prospect of the long round-trip bus ride, but there was no other responsible choice to make. And, of course, I had to admit the situation was at least partly my own fault.

Everything was calm and in order when I arrived in my ward. The patient I had worried about was sleeping peacefully in his room. He had no fever, which was a good sign. I wrote the necessary changes in medication on his chart, talked with the night nurse for a few minutes, and then left.

The air felt fresh and cool on my face as I walked outside. The buildings looked mysterious in the light of a new moon shining above the western horizon. It had rained recently, and the ground was muddy. I was glad I had on my long leather coat, which protected my clothes from the inevitable clods of black muck flung up by my boots as I walked across the yard.

The surreal form of the old broken-down trolley car loomed ahead in my path, and I had the strange feeling that it had been waiting for me. I slowed my steps as I approached, noticing that its rusting corpse looked bigger in the moonlight and that it leaned to one side. Its ancient door was open, and I had the crazy idea that it was inviting me in.

It attracted me strongly by its mysterious, dark emptiness as well as by its symbolic existence that had become so much a part of my daily life. I moved quietly closer to it. It was hard to see in the darkness, so I reached out carefully to feel for the door frame. Then I entered.

The faint moonlight illuminated only the very front part of the car, so I sat down in the driver's seat. It was hard and uncomfortable. I placed my hands on the cold steering wheel and tried to imagine myself driving this broken-down blue creature. Then I looked out through the cracked windshield to the sky. The thin crescent of the new moon was surrounded by thousands of bright, remote stars. I felt myself traveling with the bus through space in some strange, distant, and unlimited universe.

It struck me that this metaphor perfectly fitted the situation I was in. I was now the driver in charge of steering the new direction for my own life. I could choose where to go and which directions to explore, now that Umai had freed me from the tiny cell of reality I had been locked within.

Suddenly, a slight rustling sound behind me brought me instantly alert. Then a man's low voice said, "Good evening." My body went rigid with fear. Somebody was sitting in the pitch black darkness of the back row. I was totally unprotected, and we were regularly warned about fugitives from the nearby local prison. What better place to hide for the night than the trolley car? I was frozen in fear, afraid even to turn my head around.

"So, you are driving us away from all our illusions?" The question was accompanied by a familiar laugh.

"Anatoli?" I cried in relief. "Is that you?"

I turned toward the back and saw a small pinpoint of light from a cigarette. It flared briefly as he inhaled, reflecting in a familiar pair of tinted glasses and giving me a faint glimpse of Anatoli's welcome face.

"He himself," Anatoli responded.

"What are you doing here?" I couldn't hold back the question.

"Well, I guess I have a better right than you to ask this question first. I'm on duty tonight, and I escaped here for a few minutes to have a cigarette. And now it is definitely my turn to ask, What are you doing here?"

"Of course, it is you who are on duty. I should have guessed it was your night when I tried so many times to reach the doctor in charge and was told no one knew where the duty doctor was. You are famous for taking good care of your patients but being totally irresponsible when it comes to following rules and regulations. Who else would be so impossible to find while on duty?"

Anatoli laughed again. It seemed that everything that set him apart from the other doctors made him happy.

"I actually came to change the medication for one of my patients, and now I'm on my way home," I explained.

"Good for you. I am stuck here until the morning. But if you are counting on this old wreck to take you home, I think you will also be here until the morning, if not a little longer. Can I ask you another question, by the way, since we seem to be in a place of asking and answering questions?"

"You can ask, but I won't promise to answer," I replied, leaving the driver's seat and walking through the trolley car toward the back row. Perhaps because of the darkness, I experienced the illusion that the trolley car was actually moving. I even reached for the handrail for a second to brace myself, as if I was going to fall as it came to a jerky stop.

"Well, I have noticed that something is different about you ever since you returned from your trip to Altai. I don't know exactly what it is, but you are changed in some way. It's as if you have some kind of secret now, something very powerful. I have watched you writing up your diagnoses, shooting some crazy guy down with one of your deadly accurate medications, or even doing simple things like just talking to your patients and the nurses. And seriously, it seems to me that you walk inside some power that is dancing all around you.

"Everyone is talking about your miraculous successes with some of our most hopeless patients, sometimes with the help of unusual therapies that you have described as new experimental techniques but that I personally suspect come more from the ancient rather than the modern world.

"You know how obsessive I am about finding explanations for all human behavior, but this is something I can't explain at all. I guess it's none of my business, but my question is this: Is it connected somehow with Altai? That makes a personal difference for me. If you wish, I'll tell you why."

With the help of the glow from his cigarette, my eyes had finally become used to the darkness. I could see him sitting in front of me.

"Yes, it is connected with Altai," I answered him. "But I don't feel I can tell you about what happened to me there. It's not because I don't trust you. You know that isn't so. It is only because I don't feel myself ready for such explanations yet."

"I perfectly understand that. So instead of asking more about your changes, I will tell you a little bit about my own experience in Altai. If you have the time?"

"Yes. I have to catch the last bus back to Novosibirsk, but there is still time."

Anatoli had never mentioned Altai before, and I was intrigued to hear what he wanted to say.

"Well, I'm a hunter, as you know. Well, I don't mean just symbolically, as a hunter of meanings, but literally. From time to time I go to the taiga and hunt game there.

"My grandmother lives in Altai. It takes me two full days to drive to her village, so I rarely have enough time to visit. But a little over a year ago, I decided to take a short vacation and go hunting in the forest around my grandmother's village. I took my favorite rifle and went there with high expectations.

"A few days after arriving in the village, I finally went out to hunt. Winter had ended and most of the snow had melted, leaving behind a wet, golden brown carpet of last year's dead grass. Soon the new green shoots of spring would be pushing through it. The walking was easy, and I went deeper and deeper into the forest.

"You know, it's amazing what a simple change in perception can do to our minds. As I walked through the forest, I realized that just leaving behind all the noises of the big city and entering the primordial silence seemed to alter my state of mind even more greatly than some of my patients experience in the deepest stages of their hypnosis. I walked in utter silence, relaxed and absorbed within a special kind of meditation, yet still with the keenest instincts of a hunter. It was exactly what I had anticipated in going there, and I was enjoying it.

"Then a small sound on my right drew my attention. I looked, and there she was. A beautiful young deer, standing near the trees. She seemed somehow strange to me, and I knew instinctively that she would need a special strategy to be hunted.

"She stood watching me in absolute silence. She made no movements at all, but she was not immobilized by shock or fear. She was like a sculpture. Her graceful pose, her beautiful shape, could only be compared to a masterpiece of art. Every line of her body was drawn with incredible grace.

"Always before, my relationship to the animals I had hunted had been purely utilitarian. They were simply impersonal quarry, and if I could outsmart them and shoot straight, they would be food for the table. I don't know why I never saw more than this, but until that moment I had never imagined an animal could hold so much beauty.

"At the next moment my eyes met hers. Her gaze was straight and direct. I lost all track of time. I was looking into the soft black eyes of nature itself. Then something happened inside me, and I realized that it was my own eyes that were looking back at me. The boundary between me as a human being and the deer as an animal completely dissolved, and we were one. I became hunter and prey at the same time. It was real, not just something I imagined. It was a hundred times stronger than imagination. I was connected with that animal throughout every level of my entire being, from the smallest molecule to the depths of my very soul. At that moment I lost the curse of my damned rationality, my usual need to explain everything logically, to symbolize everything. It was a moment of pure, concentrated existence.

"At the next moment, my hand moved without thought and pulled back the hammer of my rifle. It was all part of the same flow of energy that connected me with the deer. It was all natural and right, because I felt both sides of what was happening. I was ready to kill, and I was ready to be killed. It was all part of the same continuum, the same balance.

"I aimed and pulled the trigger in one motion. At first I heard no sound. I saw only that this beautiful wild animal, the deer, swayed slightly and then started to sink. Every tiny fraction of her movement formed an intricately choreographed pattern, accomplished within itself, as if a set of beautiful pictures were replacing each other in my mind. And at the same time, I felt that it was me falling down, falling out of this life. Then her eyes finally closed, and the connection stopped.

"It was only then that I heard the sound of the shot, a primordial sound of life and death, a thunder filling up all the space around me. I lifted my head and looked up into the tops of the tall pine trees sur-rounding us. And then I looked at the sky. Unbelievably, there was a brilliant rainbow almost directly overhead. I was overwhelmed. I sat on the dead, wet grass and started to cry.

"I had always considered myself a very strong man, but I was cry-ing like a child. There was a mixture of pain and ecstasy in my tears, and my entire mind and body were in shock. I felt totally transformed. This was probably the only experience of my conscious life that I have never even tried to interpret or explain.

"I returned to Novosibirsk, but I was different. That feeling that came to me at the deer's death, of my heart being torn apart by the in-credibly beautiful pain of my connection with all the world around me, became a stable part of my life.

"You asked once about why I hadn't gone further with my career. I didn't answer then, but I guess tonight I have told you why. When I came back from Altai, the idea of a career had lost all importance to me. All that mattered to me was helping people through my work. Since then, every time I see a patient, I experience again the feeling of being both the hunter and the victim. This perspective colors my pro-fessional relationships. I think it makes me a little different as a psy-chiatrist. I hope it makes me a better one."

As professional colleagues, Anatoli and I were not accustomed to showing our feelings to each other too openly. I was glad he couldn't see my face clearly in the darkness. His story had made such an emo-tional impact on me that I couldn't even find the words to respond.

"Thank you for telling me your story, Anatoli," was all I was able to say. Then I remained silent for some time.

"Thank you for listening," he replied after a pause. "I told you about this only because I felt that Altai had made an important impact on you, too."

"That's right. And, like you, it still continues for me."

The sound of his voice had changed after he finished his story. I knew he was back to his usual persona as he continued to speak.

"You know, I read a lot about that place afterward. I found some great old books in a store, really old ones. Altai is one of the most mysterious and unusual regions of the world in its geography, geology, history, and multiculturalism. Many different traditions and cultures seem to have been given birth there and then spread all over Asia by outward migrations. Linguists have actually connected the Altaic language to many far distant regions. It is related to Mongolian, which is spoken from Mongolia to northern China, Afghanistan, and eastern Siberia, and to the Tungus language spoken in other parts of Siberia. The ancient Turkic languages that sweep in a huge band across the entire continent of Asia, beginning in Turkey in the west, then stretching through central Asia and western China and then reaching all the way into northeastern Siberia, also belong to the same Altaic language family.

"Can you imagine the incessant movement back and forth, the endless migrations, the innumerable risings and fallings of unknown civilizations over countless millennia, that it must have taken to leave this vast linguistic diffusion behind as its residue? I believe we will eventually discover there is something very special about Altai and that its cultural significance in human history hasn't been fully understood yet.

"I feel very angry when I see how much destruction has been done to this place. Many of the native people are alcoholics. The stores are empty of food, so on top of their regular work the people have to grow and produce their own provisions. Pollution is growing worse all the time, and I have heard they are planning to build a new nuclear power plant on the Katun River. It wouldn't surprise me to see the headless monster of our society totally destroy the treasure that is Altai within a few more decades, if not sooner."

He sighed deeply and then somehow read his watch in the darkness. "Well, we could talk more about it, but then I'm afraid you would have to stay overnight. The last bus leaves in five minutes."

"Thanks, Anatoli. I would like to stay, but my own duty night is scheduled for tomorrow. I don't feel like spending two nights in a row here, so I will say good-night. And thank you again for your story."

I left and walked toward the bus station. Turning once to look back, I saw the small flash of Anatoli's cigarette inside the dark hulk of the trolley. Somehow this little piece of light made everything around it seem alive and full of meaning.

It reminded me that the identically dark barracks of the wards surrounding and almost seeming to shelter the trolley were full of human lives. Hundreds of patients were all sleeping peacefully under this same moon, and I would never doubt again that their lives were still as full of meaning as everyone else's. We were all connected, even if this important truth was hidden for many so-called sane people.

Then I heard the sound of an approaching vehicle, and I ran quickly toward the bus stop. I knew the driver wouldn't be expecting any passengers at this late hour, so I stepped into the middle of the road to make sure he wouldn't pass by. The bus was completely empty, and I rode home in welcome silence, thinking about the unexpected miracle the evening had turned out to be.

18

Anatoli's story suggested to me that my own search for knowledge and personal growth was a drive implanted in all human beings, whether they were consciously aware of it or not. Those who were not or who perhaps felt it only from time to time might be shocked into contact with it through some unusual event like the one Anatoli had experienced in Altai. I began to observe the people around me, trying to imagine the kinds of events that might bring them into connection with their Spirit Twin and enable them to experience the miracle of life in a full sense.

The more I observed, the more convinced I became that everyone had an individual road to Belovodia. It was simply a question of being awakened to it. Unfortunately, for the vast majority, it remained totally beyond the sphere on which their daily attention was focused. The place of their Spirit Lake was completely consumed by outer needs. This seemed to burn up their life energy completely, not leaving space for even the smallest amount of inner exploration.

I became aware that this caused great suffering. Through the eyes of my own Spirit Twin, I saw how many mental problems and diseases resulted from the body's unconscious but nonetheless powerful attempts to shift its attention toward its inner needs. Unfortunately, most people continued to fight against this important transfer of energy, even in the face of serious distress, stubbornly resisting it in order to maintain their old, incomplete patterns of living.

Sometimes it took a tremendous shock to the system to move people deeply enough to upset their flawed equilibrium and steer them back to a balanced state of health. I realized that this was how Umai had treated Anna. Although Anna never showed much interest afterward in reflecting on what had happened to her, her physical health had been completely restored.

My own healing work differed for each patient, but I began to organize it in the direction of opening up my patients' minds to the inner space that existed within each of them. For many, this eventually opened a door to new powers that not only healed them but also sometimes gave them the ability to help others.

Throughout all of this, Belovodia continued to inspire me as a mysterious symbol of great significance. I was sure it represented something more than just a legend, something bigger than just a beautiful folktale. I kept turning over in my mind the specific personal connection I felt with the ancient, prehistoric Altai culture, revealed to me first through my vision of the tattooed woman, whose real historical existence had then been confirmed through the "normal" reality of her independent discovery by archaeologists. I knew that this connection was alive within me and that it was important.

The need grew within me to take another step along the path of my quest for knowledge of Belovodia. Returning so soon to Altai was out of the question because of my work schedule, so my mind turned to Dmitriev. I hadn't seen him since my experience in the mirrors, although we had talked on the phone a few times. Each time our conversation had been polite, but I had felt an awkward exchange of energy between us. It ran like a current underneath our talk, as if on a semiconscious level we were still searching for the shape and balance of our newly emerged relationship.

Our roles were complicated by the fact that Dmitriev was accustomed to being an important scientist, a national authority in his field. Yet at the time of our first meeting, I had been the authority figure, a doctor, and he had been a patient in a psychiatric hospital. Although Dmitriev definitely had broader boundaries for expressing his persona than most people, I could see that it was still important to him to be defined within the framework of his research and his academic position. Because of this there was a need to maintain a certain professional respect and distance, despite our growing friendship and my sense that we were moving toward a kind of partnership in our mutual explorations of alternative realities.

Dmitriev had been careful in our conversations not to push me toward any further involvement with his laboratory, but he always left the impression I would be welcome if I wished to return. One day I simply dialed his work number and told him that I would like to repeat my work in the mirrors if he would be willing. He agreed immediately, and we decided to meet at the institute the following day.

Spring was almost over. The trees were once again covered with green leaves, newly emerged street kiosks were offering ice cream cones to passersby, and the air was showing the first signs of the hot, heavy Siberian summer to come. The sounds of the city seemed louder than in the sleeping winter, and the people seemed to move faster and with more energy.

When I arrived at the institute, I was surprised to find Dmitriev wearing a short, newly grown beard that made him look more like a fledgling poet than an eminent scientist.

His laboratory was filled with bright sunlight coming through the windows, and it looked a little smaller to me this time. Only one of his assistants was in the laboratory, a man I hadn't seen before, who sat at his desk busily doing some paperwork. I found that I felt more comfortable with fewer people present.

As he walked with me into the room with the mirrors, Dmitriev seemed very serious, almost tense.

"I will be the only one here to work with you today," he said. Then he paused for a second. "Before we start, may I share some material with you?"

I nodded my head in agreement.

"Olga, the results of your experiment here astonished and intrigued me. I thought about your experience again and again after you left. There was much in your notes that related to the work I have been doing according to my own system of rational scientific inquiry, using conventional methods and experimental techniques. This system gave us some very interesting insights into the subjective nature of time and reality, but your purely intuitive approach led you immediately to a level we had never penetrated before. It challenged me to continue your subjective, unstructured exploration. So a few days later, I decided to conduct my own experiment with the mirrors, using your way.

"The results were fascinating and very different from anything I had experienced before. I didn't have writing material in the tube with me, as you did, but as soon as it was over I sat down and recorded everything. If you don't mind, I would like you to read my notes before you do anything yourself in the mirrors today. I think you will find they relate directly to the question you came here to explore."

"How do you know why I came?" I asked.

"Well, I can't be sure. But my guess is that you have been captivated by the mystery of Belovodia, as anyone would be who has touched it."

"Of course, you're right. That is exactly why I am here, and I would be more than interested in looking at your notes."

"Here they are," he said, handing me a notebook in a brown leather binder. "I think you might be more comfortable reading them inside the mirror."

He pointed toward the now familiar metal tube. "I will leave you here, but I will be in the next room. When you finish, let me know." He left hurriedly, before I could say anything, as if he was afraid I might change my mind.

The door closed and I was alone in the room. It was completely insulated from all outside noise, so I was in total silence, surrounded by desks piled high with books, research papers and reports. My indecisiveness about what to do next hung like a fog in the air around me.

The mirrored tube suddenly seemed intimidating. It looked like a small rocket ship, ready to transport me somewhere frighteningly remote in time and space from my present existence. Or was it some kind of strange, mechanical womb, waiting to readmit my body and return it to my place of birth?

In either case, it certainly didn't strike me as a comfortable place for reading Dmitriev's notes. I stood silently in front of it until the rational part of my mind reconquered my imagination. Dmitriev obviously must have had a reason for his suggestion, so I entered the tube, carrying his notebook with me.

I curled up like an embryo in the same position I had chosen the first time. Enough light entered through the open ends of the tube that I could read Dmitriev's notes without any difficulty.

I turned to the first page. I had never seen Dmitriev's handwriting before. He wrote in large, round letters that were easy to read.

It is eight P.M. on Friday. I have just finished my experiment in the tube. It lasted for one hour and fifteen minutes. The following records will be written in the present tense to facilitate my memory.

I enter the tube knowing that my task for today is to find and then follow Olga's path and to learn as much as I can that will extend her own exploration. I sit in my usual position, with my legs crossed. I must use the timing techniques I have learned to go back and find the exact same channel of perception she passed through.

I close my eyes and imagine the figure of my own double. He strikes the same cross-legged pose as mine, but he is sitting upside down above my head, facing in the opposite direction. The tops of our heads touch slightly. I distribute my attention equally between both figures, filling up the double with the same energy and consciousness as my usual self. Soon our joined figures begin to rotate around the connection point between our heads. From the position of my usual image, we are turning in a clockwise direction. Seen from the side, our joined shapes look like a spinning swastika. I spin faster and faster.

The piece of time I occupy is changing, going backward. My task is not to follow Olga exactly but just to find the same level of vibration she did and then see where it leads me. My inner clock knows intuitively where to stop me for this, and I trust it to do its job. I concentrate all of my attention on facilitating the wholeness of my moving image.

At some point I feel it stop. A series of energy waves travels through different parts of my body until one of them passes straight through my heart. I feel a shock, as if I have been struck by something. I remember a phrase from an ancient Coptic gospel, "You must pay attention to me in order to see me," and I know I must now direct all my attention toward this particular vibration gate. I must hold onto it without even a single moment of distraction.

I experience the familiar sensation of a new reality emerging into my perception. In the same way that a photograph gradually turns into visible shapes as it is being developed, forms and images are starting to reveal themselves for my vision. At first I see only the shapes of trees, their leaves moving slightly in the wind. Then a large courtyard reveals itself to me, surrounded on all four sides by low buildings made of reddish brown stone. I am standing in the middle of the courtyard, near a large, star-shaped flower bed filled with red and white flowers.

At first there appears to be no one else in the courtyard. I sense that the buildings are full of people and that they are working hard at creating something very significant. Then, to my right, I notice a man sitting on a bench. He is drawing something on the ground, using a long, thin stick as a tool.

The man looks very contemporary. His face seems familiar to me, but I can't remember where I have seen him before. I know from past experience that I mustn't distract myself with details like trying to remember faces. I must concentrate only on the experience of the moment.

I walk closer to the man. Lifting up his hand, he greets me with a smile. He acts as if he knows who I am, and he gestures for me to sit on the bench with him. I know that I need to be very economical with my energy to keep myself in this place, so I avoid talking and instead transfer my thoughts to him simply by looking straight at his face.

My thought to him is a question, and he nods his head as in agreement. Then he begins to speak. I hear his language as fluent Russian. "You want to hear the story of a legend," he says.

I mentally confirm this to him.

"Well, first you should consider the entire concept of a legend and try to answer the question of what separates legend from reality. Is there a difference between them? Of course, I know that at the personal level of considering a question like this you have gained a lot of freedom from your old way of seeing things, but you are still too rigid to accept that your own scientific research is a kind of legend being told by others."

I disagree strongly with this, because I feel free from any attachments at all to my position as a researcher. He pays no attention to my thought and continues.

"Now I will tell you the legend of Belovodia, only I will tell it to you not as a piece of archetypal fantasy, but as a real story. You may decide for yourself how to accept it. But what I am going to tell you is the real truth."

As he speaks, the man bends over and adds one or two small symbols to the design he has made on the ground.

"Long ago, so long ago that it doesn't make any sense to specify when, a great catastrophe shook the great continent now known as Eurasia. This catastrophe had been foreseen as a possibility by the elite inner circle of a sophisticated civilization that existed in northern Siberia. The climate then was very benign, unlike how it is today in that region. The civilization that had evolved there was highly developed. Some of their advances were later duplicated by your own culture, but in general they were more different in their skills and attainments than you could possibly imagine.

"One of the immediate effects of the catastrophe was a tremendous change in climate. Their warm, favorable weather was instantly replaced by frost. Soon the entire land was covered with ice, and it became impossible for their civilization to survive. But even after its collapse, the leading elite made all possible efforts to preserve their knowledge.

"Theirs had not been a technological culture, like yours. Their main achievements had been in developing the inner dimensions of the mind. Before the catastrophe, their entire society possessed a beautiful spiritual intensity that in your materialistic culture is experienced only by a very few. They possessed incredible psychological wisdom. They were able to control their personal experience of time, and they had learned to communicate telepathically over great distances. They had great skills in projecting the future, and their social structure was the most effective that ever existed.

"After the catastrophe, those people who were physically able were organized for a migration to the far south. The spiritual elite chose to remain behind, and these men and women experienced a series of intensive transformations. From your point of view they met death. But they still formed a collective nucleus connected with the remnants of their people who were migrating to the south.

"Those who had walked away didn't understand this fully, but they knew that their elders and teachers continued to live somewhere in the north, and they governed their lives through connections with their priests and rituals.

"Over the years the migrants' new lives became consumed by the pure demands of survival. Their memories of the past gradually faded away. With their collective attention turned toward the pressing needs of their daily material existence, the direction of their culture eventually became completely changed. But the thread connecting them with the knowledge and power of their spiritual elite has never been interrupted.

"This link is still alive, even today. But gradually, over the passage of so many thousands of years, it has become more and more hidden. Even for most of their priests, its memory manifests itself mainly in the form of legends and myths. Different names are now given to the ancient place in which the sacred knowledge is kept. Belovodia is one of them.

"Preservation of their spiritual knowledge was the goal of the spiritual elite from the very beginning of the migration. That is why they remained behind. But of course, for the spiritual knowledge to be truly alive, it must be continually integrated into the social lives of new, emerging cultures. That is how it happened for a long time.

"The migration of the original civilization, which I have told you about, was only the first one. Since then, many groups of people wandered into Siberia and were influenced by the mystical powers of the vanished civilization. The Altai region became a boiling cauldron for the creation of new cultures. Streams of humanity separated from there and traveled far in many different directions.

"One of them reached the territory of modern Iran, where the spiritual knowledge they carried with them became manifested in the birth of Zoroastrianism. Later, this same stream transferred much of its knowledge to Christianity. Another stream migrated to what is now India and Pakistan, and the establishment of a society there brought to life the treasure of the Vedic tradition. Tantric Buddhism, which gave the place of initial knowledge the name of Shambhala, was in direct communication with it for centuries. Those who went west became known as the Celts and were connected to the common source through the ceremonies of the Druids. In this way, the mystical heritage of this ancient civilization resulted in the Altai region becoming the original fountainhead for many of the world's great religions.

"There have always been people within each of these different traditions who were directly in touch with Belovodia. From time to time, knowledge from there has been opened up to your own civilization. This has happened at moments of real threat to humanity, such as the world wars. It is becoming open to you again now, because the power and energy you have accumulated are capable of causing many different kinds of catastrophes. Belovodia is becoming accessible to your consciousness to protect you by showing you other ways to live."

Then the man falls silent and starts to draw geometric figures on the ground by his feet. My perception is so overloaded from the many startling implications of his speech that I can barely concentrate enough to hold onto my presence here. I fight against my nearly overwhelming desire to jump into a discussion with him of everything he has said and of the hundreds of arguments

I want to present, and instead I try to concentrate my entire being on where I am.

From the expression on his face, I can see that he understands perfectly the struggle going on inside me.

Then he begins again, this time speaking very slowly.

"You may make the final decision about whether what I have said to you has been about legend or reality. But actually, there is no alternative except to see it as the truth that it is. This truth is a flower that has been opening its petals one by one, facilitating and supporting the beautiful treasure of human spirituality all over the planet.

"This flower is now ready to become fully open, and to be seen and understood as the blossom of all knowledge. This will happen very soon. You may respond to it in any way that you wish. You may choose to fight against it, or you may choose instead to welcome its divine essence and living beauty."

Here Dmitriev's handwriting ended, except for a few odd-looking geometric designs sketched uncertainly at the bottom of the page. His notes said nothing about his return from his experience or his reactions to it. It simply stopped, leaving me feeling astonished and overwhelmed. I understood now why Dmitriev had wanted me to sit inside the mirrors while I read his notes. It had made his experience seem so vivid and powerful that I felt as if I had made his journey right along with him.

I walked slowly to the room where Dmitriev waited, sitting at his desk reading a massive volume on physics. He stood up and immediately led me back into the privacy of the room with the mirrors.

"Well, what do you think?" he asked. He seemed excited and nervous.

"I'm overwhelmed. I don't really know what to say, except that your material completely took away my need to do something myself in the mirrors today. It perfectly answered the questions that were the reason for my visit. You were right about that."

He took a deep breath. "You know," he said, "I really have been fighting hard against the truth of this experience. I didn't even write down my reaction to it, because I was simply too confused and overwhelmed to try. At first I tried to deal with it by making it seem trivial. I told myself it was nothing more than a purely psychological creation of my own unconscious. But this didn't convince me. Then I tried to construct an intellectual argument against the whole concept, using all the information available from modern research.

"Of course, I'm neither a historian nor an anthropologist, but I have many friends in these fields. I thought I knew enough from them to reject the possibility that Siberia had ever been the home of some long-forgotten, advanced, esoteric civilization. I have even done some new research of my own on it, reading many books and articles.

"And do you know the result? I didn't find any real proof that this had actually happened, but neither was there any proof that it hadn't. In the end, the only argument to be made against it was the circular one that since it wasn't true, it couldn't be true. That's all.

"At the same time, there were many hints that supported the real existence of Belovodia and what I was told about it in my vision. There was the proven fact of Denisova's cave, one of the best-known archaeological sites in Altai, where traces of human life have been documented as belonging to the period of three hundred thousand years B.C. Then I remembered the startling comparative work that has been done between the Vedic tradition and the paganism of ancient Slavic culture. Among other things, their respective gods bore the same names and possessed similar functions.

"I even noticed that the typical hairstyle of the ancient Ukrainian Cossacks was identical to that of the modern followers of the religion of Krishna, coming from India. Both shave their entire heads, leaving only a long tail growing from the top of the crown. The followers of

Krishna believe he will pull them out of sin by this tail on the tops of their heads. I was just told by one of my friends, an anthropologist, that some Japanese expeditions were being organized to explore the territory around Altai, to test the idea that the origin of their nation could be traced there.

"It was particularly fascinating to trace the connection between the name of the principal goddess of the Altai region, Umai, and other deities such as the Indian Kali and Buddhism's Tara. I came to the conclusion that they were all one and the same. Umai was embodied in Uma, the ancient Indian female spirit, who as a Shakti of Shiva is the power of light that makes perception possible. Uma is manifested as Kali in the Kalavada system and in the Kalachakra Tantra.

"Both systems were connected with belief in a time wheel. The most sacred aspects of their rituals were the ceremonial doorways opening into the roots of time, through which the initiated ones were able to reach Shambhala, or Belovodia, and to touch the mystery of immortality. There also are striking similarities with the Zervanit tradition of ancient Persia, where the ability to understand and manipulate time was the essence of their spiritual practice.

"There are the same fascinating parallels in Sufism. For many years my good friend, Mr. Vasiliev, has led a group of scholars studying the work of Gurdjieff and his predecessors. He told me just recently that in the part of Gurdjieff's work most essentially connected to the Sufi masters, he discovered the same idea of a time wheel that could be entered and used as a passageway to the mystical gate guarding the sacred land of Hurqalya. The name *Hurqalya* can be considered as the Sufi equivalent of Belovodia.

"Vasiliev learned that Gurdjieff also found among the Sufi masters the knowledge that the time wheel represented a stable primordial law, which could be grasped and understood through many different modalities of perception. For example, the practitioner who touches this law through meditation on mandalas opens the eyes of the heart with the assistance of the visual sense. The one who listens to the music of circles, especially in the way Gurdjieff taught this, reaches the same mystical experience assisted by the auditory senses. The same state can also be reached through dance, in which the seeker's entire body becomes the instrument leading to the sacred gates.

"The group of Gurdjieff's students who remained in Russia explored this concept further. They confirmed that whatever the mechanism that is used, if it is done correctly, the time wheel will begin to spin. And it will inevitably bring us to the final point of our destination, the mystical country of Belovodia. All this is most interesting, is it not?

"Yet if there really was an ancient, advanced civilization somewhere in northern Siberia, why have we not yet uncovered its physical remains? No matter how long ago it may have existed, why does it still lie so mysteriously hidden from our view? Well, perhaps the answer to that can be found in the theories of the eminent historian and ethnologist Lev Gumilkev, whose mother, Anna Akhmatova, I consider to have been the greatest woman poet Russia has ever produced.

"While he was being held as a political prisoner in the Gulag, Gumilkev studied the effect of the cosmic laws of transformation of energy on the evolution of cultures. One of the many concepts he introduced was that every civilization is characterized by the different materials it uses as the foundations of its existence—wood, leather, fabrics, metal, bone, stone, and so forth. Because of wide variations in the materials they used as well as the climates they inhabited, different civilizations, he realized, would produce remains that would obviously be preserved very unequally.

"Civilizations relying heavily on stone and metals and existing in places with hot, dry climates would leave plentiful ruins and artifacts for future archaeologists to find. It would even be common to find well-preserved, naturally mummified human remains, as has happened in parts of Africa, South America, and the southwestern United States.

"However, cultures that used mainly perishable materials like wood, leather, and fabrics, which then were subjected to a cold, wet climate like Siberia's for many thousands of years, would leave very few traces of themselves behind. If such a civilization had also been of exceptionally great antiquity, existing perhaps not tens but even hundreds of thousands of years ago, we could hardly expect to find much physical evidence of its existence.

"So, while I cannot yet point to anything absolutely conclusive, there are many strong hints that the initial motherland for proto-Indo-European culture was not restricted to the area right around the Black Sea, as is believed by many scientists, but might be expanded to include the region of Altai as well.

"You know, Olga, altogether this has somehow worked to dissolve much of my skepticism as a scientist toward new theories that contradict accepted beliefs and that may at first seem unconventional. I no longer think it is historically impossible that Belovodia once existed and that in some unknown way it continues to exist and inform human culture.

"Maybe someday there will be hard evidence to prove this beyond a doubt to our practical, logical, scientific minds. For me, my intuition is already enough. My heart feels so happy and satisfied with the information I was given that I am ready to accept it as a belief. This is where I am so far. When you asked if you could come here again, I agreed partly in the hope that my experience could help you in your own search."

Fortunately, I had never been nearly as conditioned to believe only in empirical scientific evidence as Dmitriev appeared to have been, and many of my own stereotypes of the so-called real world had already been broken down by my own experiences in Altai. So for me, it was immediately easy and plausible to see Belovodia from the perspective suggested by Dmitriev's experience. In fact, the idea fascinated me. My reaction to it was as if I had finally received a long-awaited promise of protection and support.

I thanked Dmitriev emotionally and left feeling excited and contented. I had received everything I could possibly have hoped for from my visit. Beyond that, during my trip home I didn't devote much conscious thought to the information he had given me. It didn't really seem to facilitate rational analysis. It simply "fit" as an intuitive concept that immediately resolved many of my previous conflicts and left me feeling filled with a spiritual ease.

Once again it was late when I got home, but I decided to stay awake at least long enough to write down everything I had learned at the Institute of Nuclear Physics while it was still fresh in my mind. After I finished writing, I was more conscious than ever of the fact that my experiences were creating a new identity. This identity was steadily growing within me, becoming more and more aware of itself. I knew that this identity was connected to my Spirit Twin and that I was in the process of becoming my true self.

I felt as if I had finally connected the ends of a very important circle in my life. Later, I would learn that the search for understanding actually follows a series of circles joined together to form an ascending spiral. As soon as we have completed each turn and it has become whole within us, forming an integral part of our experience, we are immediately exposed to the outer boundary of the next circle. Then we are ready to take the spiral path leading to the next level.

Not yet knowing this, I was totally unprepared when my phone rang and my thoughts were interrupted by a man's deep, hoarse voice saying in a rather abrupt tune, "I want to speak to Olga. Are you she?"

"Yes," I answered. "Who is calling?" I was trying to recognize the harsh voice phoning at such a late hour, but it was definitely unfamiliar.

He continued in the same rude, patronizing tone, as if he hadn't even heard me. "I have been told that you are quite an interesting girl, doing quite interesting things. Aren't you?"

Then he told me his name, Mikhail Smirnov, in a way that suggested I should instantly know who he was. The name meant absolutely nothing to me, but before long I would learn he was a controversial, highly educated man who had served time in prison as a dissident and was now considered to be the godfather of all the underground esoteric and spiritual activities that went on in Novosibirsk. He had even created an international network of correspondents who sent him the latest research on human consciousness from all the corners of the world.

His call proved to be the beginning of my next circle. It would lead me back to Altai and then onward into Uzbekistan and Kazakhstan, forming a long loop in my spiral that would bring many new trials, temptations, and gifts. It would deprive some people of their sanity and even cost a few of them their lives. But it would also bring great love and peace to others. For me, it would shed more light on the tantalizing mysteries of time spirals and human evolutionary tracks, the significance of the ancient tombs with their "seemingly dead inhabitants with alive intentions," and Altai's central position in the ancient web that created so many of the world's religions. It would all be knowledge that would complete another circle in my quest for Belovodia.

Epilogue

The night sky had returned to normal, but the wind and moist air were still so refreshing that I remained on my balcony a long time, remembering the circle of dancing men and Umai's eyes at the end of my vision. looking at the stars and reflecting on the events in Altai that ultimately had changed my life in so many ways.

More than a year had passed since I had first met Umai in the village of Kubia, and I had spent much of my time traveling through central Asia in search of knowledge, meeting other new teachers in the process. Nonetheless, my memories of Umai were still alive and always brought joy and excitement. Perhaps this was because they were more than just the distant, indistinct mental pictures we usually carry through life as a record of our experiences. These memories had formed the foundation for the transformation that had taken place within me.

Although I was still absorbing and integrating into my life all that had happened in Altai and in my subsequent experiences in Dmitriev's laboratory, I had already begun making other journeys into central Asia in search of additional knowledge.

When I was beginning to write the manuscript for this book, I decided to visit Altai to ask for Umai's permission and advice. At the end of our meeting, Umai hugged me for the first time. Then she gave me a gift of some tobacco and pointedly remarked to me that the Altai name for the Great Spirit was Ulgen, which was derived from Ulkar, the Altai word for the constellation known in English as the Pleiades. When I asked her why she had told me this, she replied that she would give me no explanation. "Think about it yourself," was all she would say.

The next necessary step before publishing the book was to visit my other new teachers in Uzbekistan and Kazakhstan. One of them, who was known as the Master of Lucid Dreams, was waiting for me in the small house where we had met before.

The floor of the room we sat in was covered with soft wool rugs in red and white Uzbek designs. I felt comfortable in this room by then, so when he told me to prepare for a journey I sat down calmly near the wall in the special pose he had taught me and closed my eyes.

The trip is short, beginning with his deep, hypnotic voice saying, "I will teach you something important about your book."

Immediately I feel that he has placed an unpleasantly cool, smooth, slender, squirming object in my right hand. I start to open my hand to toss it away, but he stops me.

"Hold onto it!" he says. "Do not open your eyes! It is a snake you hold in your hand."

Whatever is in my hand is writhing furiously. I am nearly paralyzed with fear and can hardly keep myself from screaming. I still want to let it go, but I fear it is poisonous and will bite me if I do.

"Feel the snake in your hand," he says. "It is a power. Feel it and remember the sensation of holding it. You must find the balance between yourself and this power you hold. If you squeeze it too tightly, you will hurt the snake and it may bite you. If you do not hold it tightly enough, it will escape and you will lose it. You must find the correct balance and keep it."

I have tried to remember and use this lesson in writing this book. Many people are looking for power, searching for new qualities to develop in themselves, seeking to open up their own inner magic. Some will learn how to contact this inner power, sometimes very successfully. But lacking the foundation to manage and control it, they will hold it too tightly and it will bite them. Its strength will overcome them, and instead of using it they will become its servant.

People who are unbalanced in the opposing way may be capable of using their power for a while, but they will not be able to hold it and it will get away. If I have been able to transfer an understanding of the proper balance to those who read this, then one of my tasks will have been accomplished.

Before long, I will embark on my next journey. It will lead from Altai to central Asia and then to North America. It will be the same path that was walked by human beings long ago who brought the fire of truth and light wherever they went. It is the same truth and light that is returning now to the minds and memories of the people of our own time.

Introducing *Entering the Circle*, the companion CD

Also available from Triloka Records is the companion CD to *Entering the Circle* (under the same title), which features Olga Kharitidi and Jim Wilson (producer) in a tribute that remains true to the trance experience of the shamans of Siberia. The following is Olga's commentary on the making of this recording:

> *In the very depths of Siberia, in the mountains of Altai, these songs originated.*
>
> *A few years ago, a shaman came down to a remote Altai village from his unknown haven, hidden high in the mountains. Nobody ever knew where he was living. Nobody ever knew where to find him. His name, in the native language, was Kaichi, which means shaman/singer. He came down to heal people in the villages through his songs.*
>
> *Only one time did he allow his healing voice to be recorded. Sitting on the ground in the center of the village plaza, surrounded by local people who had come to listen to him in order to be healed, Kaichi sang for hours. Then he silently stood up, took up his string instrument, and disappeared. But his song traveled far away to meet with the songs and music of people from another continent and to become a message from Siberia.*
>
> *I believe that my meeting with Jim Wilson, who produced this album, was more than a happy coincidence. My entire work here in the U.S.A. is devoted to spreading the knowledge that has existed in Siberia for thousands of years, making it known as a part of the global spiritual experience. I know that this album, created by American musicians, is an important bridge connecting us with Siberia and its healers.*

Entering the Circle, the companion CD to Olga Kharitidi's book, is available from your local record store or can be ordered from Triloka Records, 306 Catron, Santa Fe, New Mexico 87501. For telephone orders, call 800-578-4419 and ask for item #EC 4109-2 for the $15.98 CD or #EC 4109-4 for the $9.98 cassette, plus $2.50 shipping and handling.